Dunfillin
Tales from the Enamel Face

OR

PNI: Laughter can seriously improve your health

Dunfillin
Tales from the Enamel Face

OR

PNI: Laughter can seriously improve your health

Lachlan B MacDonald

MÒR MEDIA LIMITED

Dunfillin
Tales from the Enamel Face

Copyright © 2019 Lachlan B MacDonald
All rights reserved.

All rights reserved. No part of this publication may be reproduced or distributed in any form or by any means, or stored in a data base or retrieval system, without the prior written permission of the author.

Lachlan B MacDonald asserts his moral right
to be identified as the author of this book.

All photographs supplied by Lachlan B MacDonald unless otherwise stated.

ISBN: 978-1-9993668-2-7

First published 2019

Mòr Media Limited
Argyll, Scotland

www.mormedia.co.uk

Cover design by Helen Crossan

DEDICATION

For Seònaid and Fionn
Brianna, Issy and Euan

ACKNOWLEDGMENTS

Kären, for producing the most amazing grandweans.

Getting things in order has always been a great strain for me and as Lillian Beckwith said in her book *The Hills is Lonely* (1959), 'the most difficult thing in the world is to form a Highland bucket chain!'

I thank all the dentists, nurses, receptionists and dental mechanics I have worked with (except one). I only had to turn up! It's the whole team that gets results, not just the dentist who—as everyone knows—are millionaires.

Many thanks to my good friend, Eilidh Crossan, without whom none of this would have seen the light of day.

My thanks to my wife Dr Diane MacDonald who corrected the grammar, spelling and accuracy when I was heading for jail, and also for big words like leitmotif, psychoneuroendocrinoimmunology, marmalade and *pull ra plug*.

CONTENTS

DEDICATION	v
ACKNOWLEDGMENTS	vii
MAPS AND ILLUSTRATIONS	xiii
INTRODUCTION	xv
Twixt Two Cultures	1
AUTOBIOGRAPHICAL	3
Teachers	7
Music	13
Perceptions of Religion (aged 10)	19
Gone Fishin'	23
Guns	31
The Ballachulish Express	35
The Ballachulish Bridge	39
Reflections on The Games	41
Hard Work, Lismore Pier	43
University Years	47
Army Days	53
Hard Work: Loch Awe	57
Dentistry I	63
The Abu Dhabi Infirmary Blues	66
Dentistry	68
Happy Days in Kirkcaldy	69
The SNP	69
The Happening	73
Dentistry II Gorbals Days	75

GÀIDHLIG — 79

    Nuair Bha Mi Òg — 83
    Lachunn a' Pheigi — 85
    Para Shandaidh — 87

BEURLA — 89

    Lachunn a' Pheigi — 91
    Para Handy — 93

ESSAYS, ARTICLES AND STORIES — 95

    Comann Eachdraidh Lios Mòr — 97
    An Sgiobair (The Captain) — 99
    The Dynamite Boats — 109
    Mo Mhàthair (My Mother) — 113
    Highland Women — 121
    Voyage to Sleat — 123
    Brine in the Blood — 125
    Diane — 129
    Seònaid — 131
    Fionn — 135
    Kären's First Sail — 139
    Grandchildren — 141
    Cars — 143
    The Beamer — 144
    Docs and Hospitals — 145
    Drink—or Long Distance Denial — 149
    Denial — 150
    Ploys — 151
    The Sayings of Grannie Brochan (Confucius of the West) — 155
    Global Warming and Climate Change — 159
    Hatches, Matches and Dispatches — 163
    Births and Christenings — 164
    Weddings — 165
    Funerals — 169
    The Funeral — 170
    Holidays and Travel — 173
    Hotels — 181
    The Police — 185
    Old Age — 193

SKETCHES	195
The Alkie	197
The Close	199
The Dug	203
LADIES I HAVE KNOWN	207
The Skiff or *Rana 1*	209
Hurley 20	209
Hurley 22 (with compliments to McGonagall)	210
On *An t-Each* (The Horse)	211
The New Boat: *Fumarole*	212
Rana 2	212
Meander: Colvic 28	213
LAN'S DITTIES, RAPS and DOGGEREL	215
A Sailing to Ireland 2006	217
Santa's a Scotsman	220
On Precenting in a Gaelic church	221
'Puter in a Surgery	221
Reflections at a Surgery Window	221
On Seeing Theresa May for the First Time, 2016	222
Theresa May, Christmas 2018	222
Theresa May 2019	222
Ah Wanna Be a Trendy Leftie	223
Rap	225
The Englander	226
REFLECTIONS	229
The MacDonald Connection	231
Closing	235
ABOUT THE AUTHOR	243

MAPS AND ILLUSTRATIONS

MAPS

1 Lismore in Alba	xix
2 Isle of Lismore (with thanks to Walter Wakeford)	xxi

ILLUSTRATIONS

3 Sports Day 1948	7
4 Margaret and I in Oban	9
5 Father, Margaret and I—all Mod winners	15
6 Stained-glass window in the Church of St Moluag	20
7 The Church of St Moluag, Lismore	21
8 Lachann Dubh's Cottage at Croggan, Loch Spelve	26
9 The Ballachulish Bridge	39
10 Lismore Pier, 1950s—after I fixed it!	44
11 Loch Awe	58
12 Entrance to Cruachan Power Station, Loch Awe	61
13 Lachlan B MacDonald, BDS	63
14 Open wide. This won't hurt a bit!	75
15 Dunfillin	78
16 Balach beag math?	84
17 An Sàilean (tràth san 20mh linn)	86
18 Ionad Naomh Moluag, Comann Eachdraidh Lios Mòr	97
19 Captain James MacDonald	99
20 Port Ramsay today	100
21 James MacDonald as a young man (assistant ferryman)	101
22 James MacDonald with Mr MacAskill the ferryman	101
23 MV *Lochnell* at Lismore Pier	106
24 SS *Lady Gertrude Cochrane*	110
25 SS *Lady Anstruther*	110
26 SS *Lady Dorothy*	111
27 Fragment of Baligrundle School photograph, 1910-11	114

28 John Buchanan, Mother, Donald Buchanan	115
29 Donald Buchanan	116
30 Margaret and AMF	118
31 Margaret (Peigi) Buchanan	119
32 All the nice girls love a sailor!	125
33 Diane MacDonald	129
34 Seònaid and AMF	131
35 Ruadh, the family dog	133
36 Seònaid MacDonald (2010)	134
37 Fionn and AMF	137
38 Fionn, Diane and Kären	138
39 Lismore Lighthouse	140
40 Isobel, Brianna and Euan	141
41 The Hairy MacDonalds: Issy, Euan, Kären, Fionn and Brianna	142
42 The *Lady Margaret* at Port Ramsay.	161
43 Seònaid and Fionn	164
44 Our wedding day at St Andrews University Chapel	166
45 Dead Centre of Lismore	170
46 Dentists in Greece	178
47 Margaret at home in Lismore	190
48 *Rana 1*	209
49 Fionn with *Salvo* (1992)	210
50 *An t-Each*	211
51 *Meander*	213
52 Robert Watt, sailing companion of many years	218
53 Eilean Munde	225
54 The nearest DNA matches so far	233
55 Who's a lucky boy then?	243

INTRODUCTION

It's great to be able to express oneself trilingually. These scribblings, in Gaelic, English and Scots, and written over a period of more than 20 years, might be of interest to dentists, sailors, connoisseurs of *uisge beatha*[1]—and children of all ages. My mind works last century (early), for which I am truly grateful.

In my life I have met:

(a) rich people
(b) intelligent people and
(c) hard people.

None of them have had to tell me they are (a), (b) or (c), because they know I know and I know they know. By the way, some of the names here have been changed to protect the guilty!

§§§§§

Psychoneuroendocrinology, psychoneuroendocrinoimmunology, or psychoneuroimmunology—abbreviated as PNI—is the scientific study of the interactions of emotions, brain and immune system, some of the body's most complex systems. Studies have proven a beneficial link between laughter and health.

In Howard Pyle's *Merry Adventures of Robin Hood*, Robin advises a young follower to 'tell us thy troubles, and speak freely. A flow of words doth ever ease the heart of sorrows; it is like opening the waste weir when the mill dam is overfull.'

PNI is one leitmotif in this book (another could be 'a Hielanman abroad'). I don't expect you to be rolling about on the floor, but if this makes someone smile, that will make me very happy.

---

[1] The water of life: whisky

§§§§§

If I have offended anyone, that was not my intention, but I should remind you that my daughter's a lawyer and gives me mates rates and, secondly, I am willing to meet anyone alone and unarmed at the place of their own choosing. No Peaky Blinders' tricks, mind.

An t-eilean àlainn san Linne Mharbhairnich,
San d'fhuair mi m' àrach nuair bha mi òg—
Nach tric mi smaointeachadh ort am aonar
Gun toir mi gràdh dhuit gach là rim bheò

> *The beautiful island in the Linn of Morvern,*
> *Where in my youth I was reared—*
> *Often I think of you when I am alone*
> *And I will love you every day of my life*

'An t-Eilean Àlainn'
Seumas Dòmhnallach

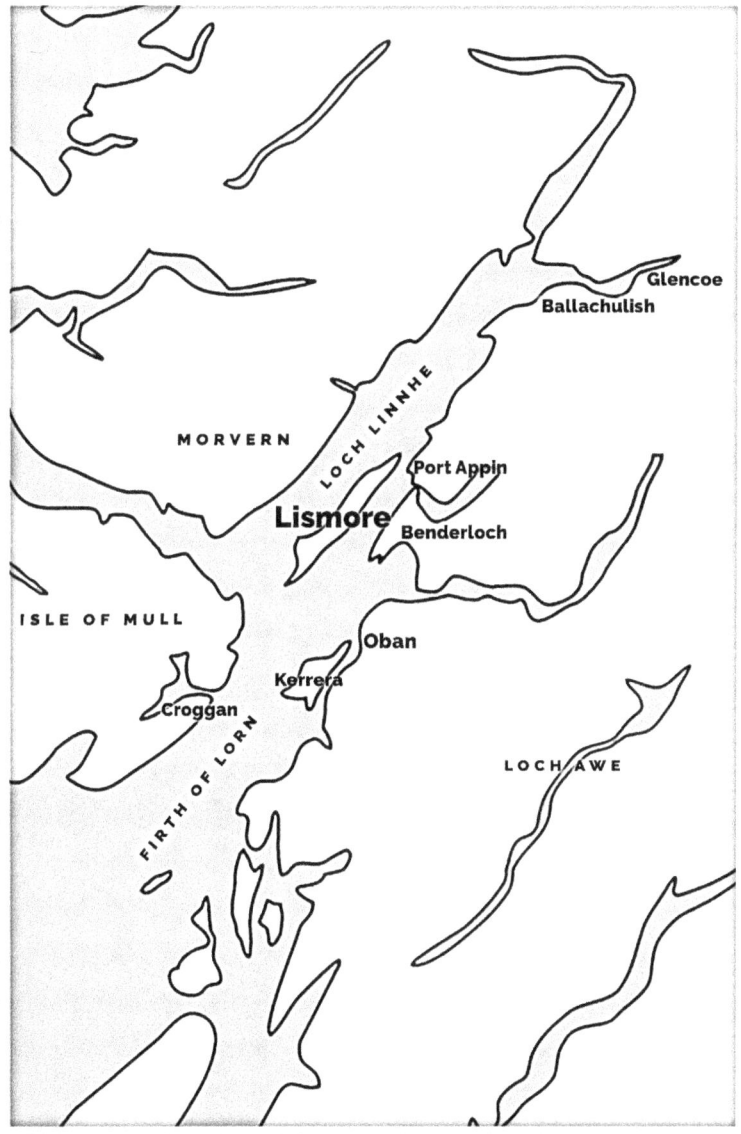

1 Lismore in Alba

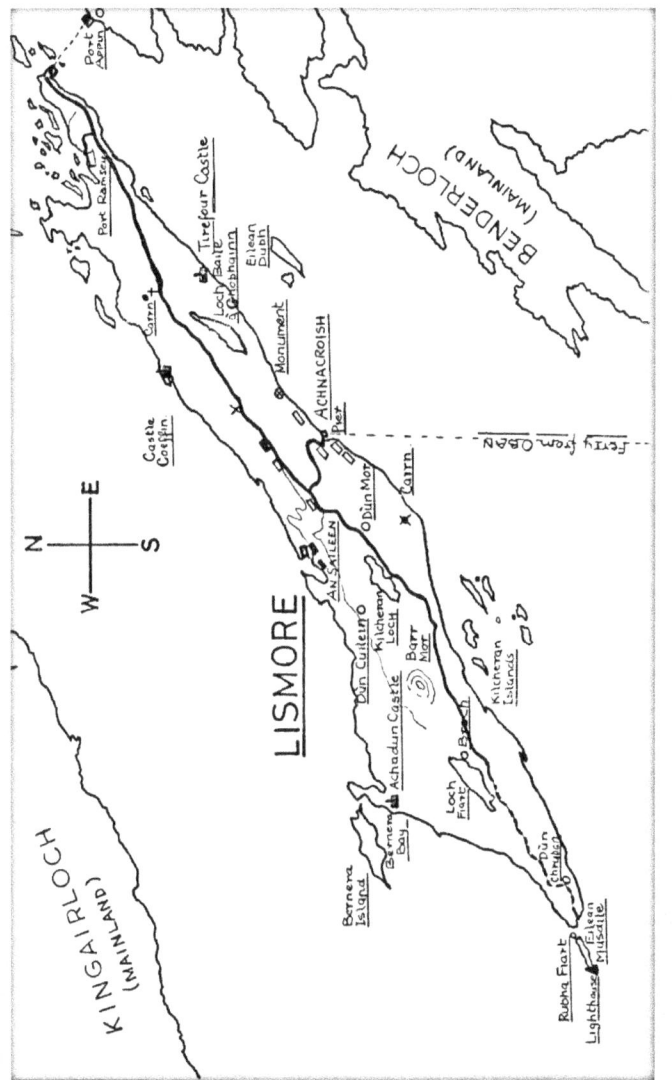

2 Isle of Lismore

Thanks to Walter Wakeford, a true British gentleman, for the hand-drawn map reproduced here

xxi

TWIXT TWO CULTURES

Thousands of people like myself who are native Gaelic speakers, i.e. learnt it at their mother's knee or some other low-down joint (the old ones are the best), do not use their native language as much as they should because they are ashamed that they do not speak it fluently enough—at least that's my excuse. It follows that the less we use it the more useless we are at using it!

In 1939, in my native island of Lismore in Argyllshire, Gaelic was the first language, but by 1945 English had gained the upper hand[1]. During the Second World War we had about 200 servicemen stationed on my native heath, some being Americans looking for R&R[2]. This had a huge effect on the language and culture, as well as on the young ladies of the island, although strangely no little treasures were left behind. I found that I could express myself quickly, easily and more colourfully in English, or the similar American form. Having to attend high school in Oban, university in St Andrews and working in England all added to the loss of my native tongue.

§§§§

Culture is defined as that which characterises a society, i.e. the social, religious, intellectual and artistic manifestations of that particular society, and of course, the language. Often by the time the importance of a native language to a specific culture is realised, much of it has been lost, even if the culture evidently lives on.

Looking at the description of a particular culture as in ethnography, you cannot see social institutions; they are not tangible things, but they are

---

[1] MacDonald, D (1994) The Cultural Construction of an Island Identity—An Ethnographic Study of an Inner Hebridean Island on the West Coast of Scotland (Doctoral Thesis, University of Stirling)
[2] rest and recuperation (also rest and relaxation; rest and recreation)

inferred from society's behaviour. Since Gaelic became fashionable and profitable, many people with no roots in Gaeldom have embraced the Gaelic language. This is not a bad thing. Wealth is important for ancient language and culture to survive, but our Celtic civilisation has suffered from a form of monetary schizophrenia for hundreds of years.

Ours is an ancient, poetic, spiritual culture in collision with that of a young, dynamic, materialistic one—*Gàidheal* versus *Gall*[3]—and because of this our language has been in terminal decline, although never quite reaching the 'almost' end, as in Cornish or Manx. All cultures need roots. A worldwide interest in all things ethnic—not least by our American cousins in search of a history for themselves—has stopped us losing our language and culture completely. The Scottish Highlander has always known that the past is important; some are just catching up.

Over centuries, the west of Scotland has been subject to waves of immigrants, making us the complex race we are now, but this pitchforking of one culture into another takes years to assimilate. We now have *Na Gàidheil Ùra*—the new Gaels—who speak Gaelic beautifully, but not all of whom have yet had the time to adjust to the cultural nuances which only time and experience can give. As the blues men say, 'if you can't feel it, you ain't got it!'

PS: I was born and raised in Lismore, went to high school in Oban and Stranraer, university in St Andrews, and worked in Corby, Northants (Little Scotland), Fife, Glasgow and Paisley. How's that for an all-round Scotsman?

---

[3] Highlander versus Lowlander (foreigner)

AUTOBIOGRAPHICAL

Nuair dh'èireas grian air sa mhadainn shamhraidh
Gur iad do chlann-sa bu mhiann bhith ann,
Ach tha iad sgaoilte air feadh an t-saoghail
'S chan eil ach caoraich ri taobh nan allt.

> *When the sun rises on a summer morning*
> *Your children would long to be there,*
> *But there are scattered worldwide*
> *And there are only sheep beside the streams.*

'An t-Eilean Àlainn'
Seumas Dòmhnallach

TEACHERS

I cannot remember being chastised unjustly by teachers or, for that matter, parents or policemen. If and when you were caught at it, which was often, you took it on the chin, you played the game and OK—you lost that round—too bad.

Parents, preachers and teachers gave children the basic guide rules to run their lives, but now the employers say that a good proportion of children cannot read, write or count properly when they leave school. If this is true, is it the teachers, pupils, parents or the system?

I had three teachers in my primary school at Baligrundle, which was a mile-and-a-half walk from my home. Often, it seemed to me as a five-year-old that it was nearer 50 miles. It was Cousin Donald who lived up the brae,

3 Sports Day 1948, with pupils from both Lismore schools, Baligrundle and Baligarve
(I am in the second row, fifth from left)

who good-naturedly gave me a piggyback when my pathetic cries of, *'Tha mo chasan beaga gort'* (my wee feet are sore) became too insistent.

When it came to sitting the quali[1], our teacher at that time did not explain what it was all about so as not to worry us. She gave me a few trial runs and said, 'I want you to try really hard tomorrow, as the school inspector may see the results.' I really liked her and did not want to get her into trouble if I blew it, so I pulled out all the stops and got good results; she was a smart woman.

At Oban High School, for some strange reason, I decided to do technical, instead of languages. As anyone who knows me will tell you, this was not smart. I am not a keen DIY chap with my trusty Black & Decker in my hand. My mother could testify to the legs on the coffee table being too close together so it would not stand alone (she kept it lovingly dusted and propped up against the wall for many years). The companion set for the fireside looked like it belonged to BC rather than AD, and if you could open the aluminium pencil case at all, your fingers were in shreds. I gave them all as presents to my mother and, God bless her, she kept the items loyally for years, and they are still in the old homestead to this very day.

In Oban High School, even Sixth Year pupils tiptoed past Room 1, where the head maths teacher ruled. He wore a smart grey suit and was built like a weightlifter with attitude.

After I had passed my Highers in Stranraer, I went back to Oban High School to study for the Higher Gaelic exam. Alongside Greek and Latin, Gaelic is recognised as a classical language (after all, it was the language of the Garden of Eden!). In those old-fashioned scholarly days you needed Higher English, a language and a science even to be considered for Uni entrance. I was amazed how the teachers had improved! It was 'Lachlan' instead of 'MacDonald', or 'boy'.

Mr T took me aside ('he's going to kill me') after I had fought the hell of Higher Maths for three months. I had barely passed Lower Maths and here I was, a stranger in a foreign land.

'Do you really need Higher Maths for university?' the man of maths asked.

'No sir, just Gaelic,' I replied.

'Better just concentrate on your Gaelic, then.'

The sun broke through and the dark clouds vanished. It was years later that I realised it was me and not the teachers that had changed. Mind you,

---

[1] the Scottish qualifying exam for streaming pupils in secondary school at age 11

4 Margaret and I in Oban

for the first three years in Oban, I did nothing apart from going to school and hanging about the lavvies with 3F (for a short time). They smoked Woodbine, masturbated and swore a lot; this swearing was new to me.

I told everyone that I was joining the Merchant Navy at 16, like many of my family before me, but I failed my colour vision test for the Nautical College. I was lost. Fortunately, my brother-in-law, Robin and my sister, Margaret—they were newly-weds—unselfishly took me to Stranraer to live with them and to sit my Highers.

Stranraer was traumatic in that I had to pack four years' work into one and the attitude was simple: work or get out. The teachers there regarded me with some confusion, as they had never met a fourth-year pupil who knew nothing. Let's face it $(a^2\text{-}b^2)$ looked like an exotic drawing to me. The maths teacher was again grey-suited (what is it with these maths teachers?), but this time he was barking mad. Nowadays he would be in a straitjacket and a Hannibal Lecter mask. After the first exam, he was belting the guys (he just ogled the girls) who only got 70% instead of 80%; when he saw my 30% he licked his lips and tightened the grip on his Lochgelly Special[2], but I said in a calm, fearless voice (people often behaved like that when they stepped up

---

[2] famous makers of teachers' punishment leather belts

to the block), 'It's senseless to belt me, as I cannot do maths, but I am willing to do extra lessons.'

He reeled back as though shot, and pale to the gills, he muttered, 'Go away boy, go away.'

The science teacher was very small and sniffed constantly, and my take on him was that he came from a poor family who could not afford handkerchiefs.

To pass the time after we sat our Highers, we listened to a science programme on an old radio that shrieked occasionally. My mate Kenny and I practised till we got the pitch right. We sat on either side of the class and joined in with the radio. This drove the teacher mad until one day I got the pitch wrong, and was rewarded with six of the best. The only thing that worried me about the belt was that I would get something in my eye, and the class would think I was crying! Those were the macho days. Nowadays, you have to show your feminine side and greet[3] on all occasions. Look at the soccer players: it's only a matter of time before they are fornicating on the touchline after scoring a goal.

I had free periods of time. There was no Gaelic in Stranraer—they spoke Galway Irish there—so I studied music for a short time. I was the only boy in the class; the girls had been doing music since they were born. Duggie the music teacher said to me one day,

'What's your instrument, MacDonald?'

'My voice,' I said.

I started to sing, but after the second verse of 'The Highland Tinker', he chased me out of the music room.

Mr Ball the English teacher opened my mind to English literature, especially poetry—I even liked Chaucer.

After I got my Highers, he asked my brother-in-law Robin what I was going to do at university; Robin said that it was dentistry.

'That's a good job,' he said, 'but it's a pity about Lachlan's education.' He was not a nasty man. I love telling this tale to my dental colleagues! My father (born in 1885) thought that barber surgeons were good only for a haircut and a tooth extraction.

(As an aside, at university we had a chap from Oz whom—with amazing originality—we called Digger. In St Andrews for the first two years, medics and dentals did the same subjects and then went their separate ways. At the

---

[3] cry

end of the first two years' dental course, the prof sent for Iain, told him he was too intelligent for dentistry and Iain ended up a brain surgeon in Oz, USA and China!)

Another star at this time was 'wee Wally', who had the frame of a 12-year-old and the genitalia of a porn star. 'Do it, do it, do it!' was the cry as the ring of cheering scholars gathered around him in the toilets; Wally would 'do it' at the drop of a hat and with great gusto. He was last seen being led away covered with a raincoat by two teachers to the Argyll and Bute Hospital in Lochgilphead. I trust he found success in his chosen profession.

§§§§§

The old saying 'if you can't do it, teach it' is a bit mean. In a sink estate school, where the little darlings drink, do drugs and are tooled-up, teaching is not an easy job. Even in my youth, a *weel-kent* face in Oban, who became a teacher, had his problems. After spending 40 minutes on the cereal crops of the USA, he asked the class to name one cereal crop from the USA.

The wee one who sat at the front and wanted to be loved said in all seriousness, 'Please sir, bananas.'

'Bananas, my f****** a***!'

He resigned the next day, and took over running the family hotel.

Ah well, another day, another dollar!

MUSIC

If music be the food of love—rock on!

They wrote poems, made songs, played instruments and sang like linties[1]; mine was a musical family with a capital M, and I couldn't even whistle. My grandfather, father and uncles were bards, played instruments and performed; my mother and sister were lovely singers. I thought I had cracked it with the Jew's harp, but the bloody thing hurt my teeth.

For some reason, I was terrified of the bagpipes; Mother had to remove me from the hall when the war pipes were produced. What a redder for the family!

Our family pipes stayed under the 'wee room' bed and guess who slept there? Their home was in a wooden case which bore a striking resemblance to a child's coffin (just my size). In the night the lid would open with a rusty metallic squeal and the multi-limbed tartan-clad horrors would drag themselves moaning and groaning over the linoleum towards me. Grabbing the twelve-bore, which also lived under the bed, I gave them both barrels and blew them to smithereens. In the silence that followed, my mother would cry out,

'Dè an diabhal a tha thu a' dèanamh?' (What the devil are you doing?)

'Just a bit of wind, Mother,' I'd reply.

You develop a magnificent imagination when you're on your own with no-one to play with.

Cousins and friends would come to enter our own bagpipe competitions as to who could play the longest. The kitchen was small: three strides and bang into the jawbox[2], about turn and three back into the dresser. The noise

---

[1] linnets
[2] large, deep kitchen sink, also known as a Belfast sink

was appalling, and I could not escape, as it was night outside and upstairs was dark—no way. I knew fine that *bòcain*[3] lurked in the corners. Would it never stop? The performers would seem to be getting tired, then mother would say that it was lovely and could she have another tune, please? I know how to make terrorists talk.

§§§§§

At my son's wedding in a small Somerset village, an ancient local watched as his church was submerged in tartan, heather and bare-ar**ed kilted *Hielanders*. As my wife's cousin tuned up his war pipes (they are gifted too, dammit), the local's head turned and he said, 'I loik the Scots, but I don't loik the way they treat their animals.' I kissed him on both cheeks in the Gallic (not the Gaelic) fashion.

§§§§§

My father and my sister dashed about at Mods (Gaelic music festivals sometimes known as the Whisky Olympics) singing in flash halls whilst mother and I stayed at home in the cinders (spot the big R—resentment!). With no electricity until 1970, it was up to ourselves to find entertainment. Mother and I would play poker or arm-wrestle—Mother always won!

Mother secretly entered me into, and coached me for, a Mod competition. On the big day when the programme came out, Father was surprised and apprehensive; he didn't think I could sing. But that day, I won a second prize and so I spent the next winter standing at the top of the stairs singing the mucous membrane off my throat. Father loved a winner.

That year I had two firsts, then it all went wrong as I entered puberty, my testicles dropped and my voice broke. I was second last and Father lost interest. But there were no regrets, as a photo of Father, Margaret and I—all winners—beams out from the mantelpiece. Mother should have been there too, but she was a retiring soul.

---

[3] ghosts

5 Father, Margaret and I—all Mod winners

My uncle John MacDonald, or 'Lismore' as he was known in Gaelic circles, was a big man with shrapnel in him who did not suffer fools lightly, and was at war with wee, less talented people in *An Comunn Gàidhealach*[4] for most of his life. In the 1920s, he was way ahead in the final of the Gold Medal and had just finished singing—by all accounts brilliantly—his own song, and striding to the front of the platform addressed the adjudicators thus: 'Wouldn't you be the proud men today if you could write and sing a song like that?' He came second—surprise, surprise. The song? *'Muile nam Fuar-Bheann Mòr'*[5].

§§§§

The next attempt to enter into the world of music was a Premier drum kit bought from a Welshman at university in the early 1960s. It had a three-foot high bass drum—the ones you see in the black and white movies of the 1920s—and even with two dampers it shook the plaster off the walls. I moved digs a lot that year. I linked up with other student music-makers, and we had piano, tenor sax, Bb clarinet, banjo and drums. We were offered a gig at the students' union once, but no-one said, 'Wax it, it'll sell a million

---

[4] The Highland Association
[5] Mull of the Big Cold Bens

copies!' I sold that drum kit one summer to buy two or three drinks and a train ticket home.

§§§§

Becoming more responsible as a professional man, I enjoyed some New Town[6] ceilidhs with good friends. Jim had a fiddle and his best piece was 'The Hen's March to the Midden'—not a propitious start. I sang heartily along, accompanying myself with the bongos. It gave 'MacPherson's Rant' a whole new sound. At one Burns supper where they were aficionados, I felt obliged to entertain them with my spiel about Rabbie on remembering what he wrote about the Highlands, on visiting Inveraray.

There's naething here but Highland pride,
And Highland scab and hunger:
If Providence has sent me here,
'Twas surely in his anger.

As a man who doesn't harbour resentment, I then went on to sing two Gaelic songs, and ended with the following gag.
'Rabbie was successful in most fields. He was a religious farmer; after sowing his wild oats, he came home and prayed for crop failure. He was blessed with fruitful women and cursed with barren land. If it had been the other way about, no-one would ever have heard of him.'
Jim, in a burst of enthusiasm, sweaty hands and Johnnie Walker (or as Rabbie would say, John Barleycorn), lost hold of his bow, and hit the *Fear an Taighe*[7] in the ear. We had the audience right behind us; fortunately, we reached the railway station before they did.

§§§§

Down in Glasgow, I was thrown out of a Rangers pub after a surreal argument with the bouncers who thought I was Irish when I started singing Gaelic, and therefore a Celtic supporter. I thought I got the bum's rush for not being good enough.

---

[6] Glenrothes, not Edinburgh!
[7] Chairman

But it was good in Glasgow; I had great times with the Govan Gaelic Choir. My loudest cheer came when I was last on in the bass section, so I was first off. I got lost backstage and marched back on the stage with the choir following along behind me, leading to much amusement and rapturous applause as we all marched across the stage and off the other side.

I hired a large hall to have a charity do; it was too large, the piano was locked, the tenor had a temperamental (half 'temper' and half 'mental') boyfriend, and someone produced a demented box-player with no finesse. For reasons beyond imagination, I did the longest three-minute set in my life on the *svarabhakti* vowel in the Indo-European tradition to an audience that had been trawled from the lower end of the gene pool. Coming off stage in a lather of sweat, I said to the box-player, 'Man, I was dying up there.'

'You certainly were, my son' said he with no sympathy whatsoever.

Should I punch him, go home or burst into tears?

The show must go on; I staggered through it.

§§§§§

By now becoming international, I sang at a ceilidh on the Great Barrier Reef and had a local to back me on the didgeridoo in Karunga, Australia. That particular instrument works well with *'Fonn air a' Ghille Dhonn'* (a reel). There was great *craic*[8] to be had at Jōetsu City in Japan at a karaoke when I modestly announced to the puzzled Japanese audience of two hundred that I knew the tune and the words for a march, strathspey and reel, so didn't need their machine.

§§§§§

Over the years, music has given me much pleasure, whether it be light classical, Gaelic, Scottish dance bands, R&B, jazz, country and western, blues; but please no dirty rap or modern jazz[9]!

The so-called rap of our American cousins comes directly from our rellies[10] in Port Ramsay, Lismore, Argyllshire. The most famous of them were the MacDonald brothers, James, John and Lachie, who specialised in a form

---

[8] Fun, good conversation, socialising

[9] Although I have actually included a rap of my own later in this volume.

[10] relatives

of rap, or *port-à-beul*[11] accompanied by a Jew's harp and foot-stamping. They are best remembered for 'Staffa Rappa' (a version of this was recorded some years ago by a German composer chappie visiting the West Coast), 'Black Tobacco Chows' and the punters' favourite, 'Big Mary's Farewell to the Whisky', the latter only failing to get into the top 20 by a whisker and still a big hit at ceilidhs, Bar Mitzvahs and AA meetings: *'Cha ghabh mi dram; cha ghabh mi dram, Cha ghabh mi dram no more'*. I suppose there is a link with dentistry: gargling is in our oral tradition.

When you get older and your ancestors come to call, I do ask: 'Dear God, let them be bagpipe-free!'

---

[11] mouth music of the Gaels

PERCEPTIONS OF RELIGION (AGED 10)

On Lismore, there were two impressive churches; Clachan is the 6th century Church of St Moluag, who was a bishop (Columba, also of saintly fame, was only an abbot). Not many people have heard of Moluag; Columba had a better PR system[1]. There was also a United Free church, which figured largely in my childhood perceptions of religion.

We went to both, which was unusual: the Church of Scotland at Clachan and the United Free Church of Scotland at Baligrundle at the opposite end of the island. Father would have gone to a mosque if there was one. 'All rivers run to the sea' was his motto. He was the precentor of the Gaelic psalms in Clachan on a Sunday and on some wet dreich winter mornings, Rabbie Burns' poem rang true: 'As cauld a wind as ever blew'. The minister, Reverend Ian Carmichael, DSO, MC, MA, author of the famous book, *Lismore in Alba*, came from an old, distinguished Lismore family. He was a leader of men on the battlefield and in the pulpit.

It was better in the summer evenings when mother and I walked up the *Aonaidh*[2] and into the church. The dust motes danced in the shaft of light through the stained-glass windows; the one with Jesus holding the lamb and with the setting sun forming a crown about his head was my favourite.

---

[1] Adamnán of Iona
[2] Shore path

6 Stained-glass window in the Church of St Moluag

The beadle was a big man with a dark suit, close-cropped hair and size 12 boots. He pulled the bell with the strength of fifty years of farming behind him, putting the bell tower in jeopardy; plaster fell as we passed. He took the collection with half-decked boxes on long poles that he pushed close to the congregation's collective chests. Father said he kept a weather eye out for farthings and buttons. Ponderously he carried the communal bible, which weighed about half a hundredweight, up to the pulpit and dropped it from a great height onto the lectern. It crashed down and the dust rose for all to see.

The minister was then herded into the pulpit and the door closed behind him with a thud; bang went the bolt and, with a satisfied sigh of a job well done, the beadle tramped heavily back down the pulpit stairs.

'Mammy, Mammy,' I said. 'Why is he locking the minister in?'

'*Wheesht, a laochain.*' (Hush, my little hero.)

I never did find out!

About the age of ten, for no apparent reason, I decided to stop going to church. Mother made sure I was dressed in kilt and jersey before getting herself ready (Father dressed himself). This gave me the opportunity on subsequent Sundays to:

- jump into the North Atlantic (a kilt spreads out like a gorgeous multi-coloured water lily)
- immerse myself in *Tobair an Iasgair* (The Fisherman's Well)
- jump into a shallow bog on my way to church.

Clothes were in short supply, so 'silly boy' had to stay at home—terrific!

Of course, the parents figured it out and the next Sunday I was driven gently like a young stirk between the barbed-wire fences on the main road to Peter MacPhail's United Free church. I constantly tested the parameters, but when I kept hitting brick walls, I changed course and went with the flow. Nowadays I would be up to my ears in child psychologists, counsellors and pills.

Often on Sundays we went to see Donald and Jessie Buchanan in *Sàilean* on the other side of Lismore and on the way back from there called at the United Free church for a sermon. Mind you, an hour is a long time for a wee

7 The Church of St Moluag, Lismore

boy in church, straining at the leash and with a head full of ploys, but this was more like it. There was no organ, so the minister led the singing with the help of his brother-in-law who loved music. To my greater enjoyment, and to the lesser enjoyment of the congregation, every psalm was embraced with the full volume of his lungs—which was considerable. That, alongside the noise of the woman next to us who had a voice like a crosscut hitting a rusty nail—wow! Not to be outdone, I opened up the throttle on my own vocal chords. Unfairly, in my eyes anyway, I was reined in by the pursing of my mother's lips and a small but disapproving shake of that auburn head.

Just before the sermon, while the collection is being taken, the ministers always mug up on their sermon. At this point Peter the Minister would disappear from view. Whether the stool was too low or the pulpit sides too high, we lost sight of him for a bit.

I asked, *'Càit a bheil e nis?'* (Where is he now?)

The response from Father came back.

'He's got a trap door in the pulpit that leads to the manse and he's away to put on the potatoes. Watch you, the sermon will end in twenty minutes.'

And sure enough, in the time it took the potatoes to boil, we'd be out of there.

Remembering this years later and as a grown man at university and still desperate to know the truth, I sneaked in one night to look, knowing of course that it was only a joke, wasn't it? How I would have loved it to be true.

GONE FISHIN'

My great-grandfather, *Lachunn Dubh*, from Mull was jailed for fishing; my maternal grandfather from Lismore was drowned fishing; my father was good at fishing and I'm pretty keen myself. *Lachunn Dubh* was very fond of young ladies, and of fresh salmon (or was it the other way around?). He also wrote a song called *'Am Ministear 's am Bàillidh'* in which he wished they would behead the water bailiff and put the minister to death, which resulted in him being banned from the church, yet again.

Fishing was a serious business and the sport involved certainly came second to the protein factor. Things were sombre until you had caught your breakfast, then the *bodaich*[1] relaxed and lit up their pipes. Although we fly-fished the loch for trout, most of the fish taken were saltwater, i.e. *rionnaich* (mackerel), *cudainnean* (cuddies) and *piocaich* (saithe).

The method used was for the person fishing to sit on a plank over the gunwale, with his feet in the stem sheets, a rod on either shoulder, one under each thigh and two line spinners running wide. This gave more coverage, but woe betide you if the mackerel hit and you landed with a ball of twine at your feet as all the lines became fankled[2].

Women did not go fishing, and it was unlucky to meet a woman on the way there, especially if she had red (or reddish) hair, as had my mother. One evening she ran out to save the washing on the line from a shower of rain and met John with his rods on his shoulder.

'Oh tha mi duilich, a Sheonaidh,' thuirt ise. ('Sorry John,' she said.)
'Ceart gu leòr, a Pheigi,' thuirt esan. ('It's OK, Peggy,' said he.)
And John turned on his heel and went home.

---

[1] older gentlemen
[2] entangled

§§§§§

Fishing was not on the agenda on Sundays, but when Father rowed us up to Stronacraoibh on a Saturday (we walked the half mile from there to Port Ramsay to see Jock and Jessie), we would trail a fishing line, and mother, too, was allowed. Right under the Broch, the line went to the bottom; it was a big one. Father went into high instruction mode.

'It's big! Keep the line taut! Don't jerk! It's got a soft mouth! Fingers in the gills as it comes over the side! Get the tackle back into the water fast, it will have a mate!'

Mother, totally flustered but willing to try hard, unhooked the fish in a trice with great efficiency, threw the tackle into the bottom of the boat and the fish over the side! Father never said a word, but bowed his head and kept on rowing; only I could see the veins standing out on his neck.

§§§§§

Children did not go fishing until they were old enough to row. When my Uncle Lachie came on holidays, to 'please the wee boy', he would take me out fishing in the middle of the day. Under the Mill at Balnagown, with the sun splitting the heavens, we hit an eye of saithe lying there in a huge breeding mass and in ten minutes had a basketful.

'Don't tell your Father where we got them and he'll just stop short of torture to get the information out of you,' Uncle said.

My lips were sealed and every night Father and chum went looking for the spot with no luck and Uncle Lachie and I came home every lunchtime laden with fish. I was worried.

'He'll follow us up the shore and find out our secret place.'

'No, he's too proud to do that, but you might see the flash of the binoculars.' He knew his brother well.

We kept the place a secret and named the wee bay *Camus Lachuinn*.

§§§§§

A huge retired miner from Glasgow came to stay next door and was 'angling' to go fishing with Father, who would have none of it.

'*Seall air na casan air—tha e spàgach* (look at the size of his splayed feet), and if he goes over the side, we're drowned.'

At that time no-one fished off the Pier as it was where we drowned cats and dogs. From somewhere the *bodach*[3] got a rod the size of a Christmas tree. Father found this hilarious.

'He'll be using a heaving line and an anchor as tackle and I hope to God he doesn't fall over the Pier and drown.'

On the second cast the *bodach* pulled out the biggest lythe[4] we had ever seen.

'Daddy, Daddy, Mr Sellar's caught a monster.'

No jokes now from father, who was very competitive.

The next time Father was in Oban, one of the reporters from the Oban Times asked him if there were any hatches, matches or dispatches from Lismore.

'No,' said father, 'but a big miner from Glasgow caught and ate the children's pet fish. It was so tame that in the winter it would put its head up on the seaweed and the children would feed it with crusts.'

'Glasgow Man Eats Children's Fish' roared the headline, and that was the end of Mr Sellar's fishing. The rod rotted at the end of the house.

'*A Sheumais, Sheumais, nach robh thu cunnartach?*' (James, James you larrikin!)

§§§§

I bought a splash net one morning. Neil and I went fishing up the Sound of Mull. Neil cannot tell you how he knows where the fish are; he has an instinct, an intuitive feel for it, from his forebears. We landed two queer fellows; Neil never uses the word salmon. We went into Lochaline for the night and dammit—there was the Fisheries' cruiser. Fortunately, they are not suspicious of yachts, so I anchored close and had a shouted conversation:

'Busy these days?'

'Yes, indeed. Six illegal nets this week.'

'It will be the tourists.'

'Bugger the tourists, it's the bloody natives!'

(The native is standing on a net and two salmon!)

Landing Neil next day so he could get back to his scrap business, I was lying in the stern, fishing, with a hot sun high in the sky. I opened a five-

---

[3] old man
[4] *Pollachius pollachius*, known elsewhere as pollack

8 Lachann Dubh's Cottage at Croggan, Loch Spelve

gallon petrol can, which vomited petrol into the cabin and, as I had just cooked a meal on the stove, that pre-explosion haze appeared. I was about to leap into the rubber boat when valour overcame common sense and I opened all the hatches and threw a bucket of water over the stove.

Excitement over, I began to wonder: if I had thrown a lighted fag end into the cabin, I would get the insurance, which was more than the yacht was worth. Bad idea; I'd probably get burned to death, drown or be jailed. I headed up Loch Spelve, past the ruins of Great-grandfather's house at Croggan, wishing him good luck, wherever he was (he died in 1902) and dropped anchor beside another yacht.

'Fancy a cup of tea?' came the call.

This was in the olden days when boatmen spoke to each other. I went over to regale the chap with details of poaching salmon, and of contemplating setting fire to my yacht to get the insurance. I was of course, hyper after all the excitement and after a time, I noticed that my companion had gone very quiet.

'Where are you from, and what do you do?' I asked cheerily.

The answer: 'I am an inspector in the Strathclyde Police.'

'And I am the biggest liar in *Earra-Ghàidheal*[5]!' I said quickly with a strangled laugh.

But things were a bit strained after that and I took my leave, and left very early the next morning.

§§§§§

In the days when I took a small refreshment and had partaken of a splendid lunch with some hooligan friends in Oban, I went down to board the ferry. They had just started the roll-on roll-off ferries known as ro-ros. There I found this chap in a shooting brake (estate car) looking lost and confused.

'Which boat are you looking for?' I asked, being helpful.

'The Lismore boat,' he told me.

So I showed him to the correct boat and started chatting with him. I noticed he had fishing rods in his car so I started to impart my valuable local knowledge by telling him where the best fishing was to be found on Lismore.

'Use Balnagown loch, it's the best, but don't go over to *Coille nam Bàrd* side, you are too exposed there. Go past the waterfall on the west side; it's the best spot. They cannot see you from the road there. Also, if you're worried about the Fells, the owners, phone at 8 a.m.. If no-one answers, you're OK.'

The chap was not big on conversation, so I carried on by asking where he was staying for his visit. The answer was *Uamh Nèill*[6]. This was no less than Major Fell himself. I had spent the last ten minutes telling the man how to poach his own trout in his own loch. (The only poaching I recognise is breaking an egg and dropping it into boiling water.) With luck, the Major dined out on this story. I certainly did.

§§§§§

I stayed in the East of Scotland—Angus and Fife—for 20 years and got to know the fishermen of the East Neuk. True Fifers, Willie and his forebears had fished the dangerous east coast for generations; at least in the west you can hide behind an island.

---

[5] Argyll
[6] the big house near the north end of Lismore (literally Neil's Cave)

A friend James and I met the crew in Pittenweem as they boarded early in the cold dark of a February morning, with an easterly that penetrates the very centre of your being. The engineer stopped and regarded us in our sailing gear.

'*Are ye the lauddies that are goin' fishin' wi' us the day?*'

'*Aye.*'

'*Dae ye mean ye goat oot yer baids at fower i' the mornin' tae gae fishin' wi' us?*'

'*Aye.*'

'*Ye must be bluidy maaaaaad!*'

As we steamed out to the fishing grounds with the skipper at the wheel, I regaled the crew with tales of derring-do on the West Coast. The forecastle was small and smelt of diesel oil, old fish and blocked lavatories; the food consisted entirely of hard-boiled eggs in rolls and cups of tea that had the consistency of hot syrup, while the boat seemed to climb forever, and then freefall off the side of a cliff in the heavy seas.

'*Make way for the lauddie,*' cried the engineer with some satisfaction, as my face went white, the world revolved and I made a dash for the deck.

The gale came suddenly with a trawl still down, and I thought each time she would not be able to lift her stern with the crew up to their waist in water, but she did.

We made for Methil, and I noticed one boat wallowing as another circled her.

'He's got a line round his prop,' Willie explained.

'Shall we call the lifeboat?' I asked. Willie looked as though I had hit him.

'*Whit fur? His brither Tam's wi' 'im,*' as if Tam and the Almighty were on nodding terms.

Brother Tam was in the circling boat and, having provided practical assistance rather than prayers, they both steamed into Methil an hour or two later.

A hugely intelligent man with a Fifer's gift of throwaway humour, Willie represented the East Neuk fishermen at a meeting in Edinburgh of politicians, advertising and moneymen with Sir John Gilmour, MP for North Fife chairing a meeting on the subject of sewage in the River Forth. The joke going around at that time was that if you fell into the Forth, you didn't so much swim as just go through the motions.

They spoke all day of sewage, effluent and discharge without coming to any conclusion. It was approaching five o'clock; Willie needed his tea and was fed up to the teeth with all the talk. Rising from his chair, he addressed the chairman in that familiar yet polite fashion of our forefathers:

'Aye, aye, Sir Joahn, we ken aw' that, but whit are ye goin' tae dae aboot the shite roond the Mey island.'

The suits folded their jotters and went home; they didn't have a clue.

§§§§§

For all sorts of reasons, the fish numbers are declining on both east and west coasts. I'm getting old, and it's no longer the poor man's food. It is only a matter of time before the government bans fishing altogether. Ach well, two-thirds of the important decisions are made in Brussels and the rest at Westminster.[7] Maybe you have to ban things like foxhunting and fags just to pass the time. More and more restrictions are placed on the professional classes by the inadequates who laughingly call themselves politicians.

---

[7] Of course, this may have changed by the time you read this!

GUNS

As with fishing, it was protein first and sport second. My father used to provide us with geese, duck, hare and the occasional hind from Kingairloch. My father had a bigger effect on me than I realised.

Father was a skipper in the Merchant Navy, and often sailed in and out of Hamburg in Germany. He bought his gun in a pawn shop there. It had belonged to a local poacher who had fallen on hard times. It was a side-by-side twelve-bore, with outside hammers and a long Damascus barrel. You could pull both triggers and hardly feel the kick. If I had tried that with the ruskie I had years later, I would have landed flat on my back.

My uncle Lachie, also a skipper in the Merchant Navy, once had to retrieve a .303 rifle from his drunken cook who let off a round on the SS *Lady Dorothy*. Pretty upsetting for my uncle; his boat was one of the three ICI boats which sailed from Irvine to Hamburg carrying high explosives. Lachie gave the .303 to my father after he (my father) retired through ill-health as the skipper of the SS *Lady Gertrude Cochrane*; he now had a new role as captain of the Home Guard.

This was a single shot Winchester action·.303 Lee Enfield for holstering in the saddle of a horse and had allegedly seen action in the Boer War. It was amazingly accurate and after it stopped killing deer, it was used to welcome in the New Year at Achnacroish.

As a teenager, I was at target practice on the Black Isle[1], and before getting into the skiff I carelessly let one off into the water. Lismore is only half a mile away, the bullet ricocheted off the water—now spinning and the size of a new 50p piece—and just missed the local farmer who was leading a cow to the bull on the larger island; a close shave indeed.

---

[1] a small uninhabited island off Lismore

I knew nothing of this until a month or so later at a dance on Lismore when the farmer, a smart, quietly-spoken man, approached me and said, 'Be more careful with that gun, Lan. I'm not going to tell your father this time!'

I certainly took his advice, but that was how we were in those days.

The same farmer, when he heard that a chap was smoking wacky baccy, said that he did not want drugs on Lismore. The accused said that there were a lot of drugs already on Lismore.

'What do you mean?'

'Whisky.'

'That's not a drug.'

The next day, the farmer apologised and said he had never realised that whisky was a drug. Ditto.

My father was very careful about breaking the gun, taking shells out, keeping safety catches on, and taught me a fundamental lesson one day. After pleading and pestering for years, I finally persuaded him to give me a .177 Diana air rifle which could hardly punch a hole in a cardboard box. One day, I pointed my new weapon at my father across the garden. There was no pellet in it, but I was unpleasantly surprised that a 65-year-old man could travel so fast across the garden.

'Do not point a gun at anyone unless you're going to kill them,' was the message that day. The only other time Pops (as I called him—Popeye the sailor man) chastised me was when as a little boy, I kept sticking my fingers in front of the saw as he was cutting logs. After telling me to stop it a few times, he picked me up and skelped my *tòn*[2]! Nowadays, Pops would be up for child abuse but I have never stuck my finger in front of a saw again. Things were tough back on the croft!

§§§§

An acquaintance from university came over to the island for a weekend. He said he could get a Bren gun as he was a member of the OTC[3], but I persuaded him a .22 would do. I knew he would not hit anything as he loved the noise of the bang, but shut both eyes when he pulled the trigger. We left for the islands off the coast with the .303, the .22, the shotgun and the Diana air rifle for show. We had the rest of the guns in the boat and, going past the

---

[2] backside
[3] (University) Officers' Training Corps

window, I waved the airgun to show Mother how responsible I was! First off in the skiff, my companion pulled the .22 across me and squeezed off a shot, obviously no safety on! I explained about the wee hole going in and the big one coming out, but he was not impressed. He had secreted some .303 shells on his person (again with only half a mile from people) and he let one off above me on the beach. A bullet coming close does make a noise like a hornet. I searched him, removed all ammo from his person and we moved to another island in the group. We went ashore and I went up the hill to look for rabbits.

It being a dry spring, the island was like a tinderbox, so the bold boy walked along the shore, setting fire to the bracken, and with me up on the cliffs to the leeward side. Smoke-blackened, with my nerves in tatters and worried about my parents, the police, the coastguard and the men in white coats, I managed to get us back to the homestead with the arsonist giggling in the stern of the boat and me with an oar in my hand promising to split his skull if he made any false moves.

Far from finished, he attempted to blow the coal fire out with a home-made bomb (it didn't go off), and the next morning put a hole in my grandpa's ship's bell which was hanging from a tree at the bottom of the garden. This was my father's pride and joy, and this was the only target my visitor had ever hit in his life. The shooter was off on the next boat!

§§§§§

Growing up on the island you could shoot almost anywhere and drop something off at the house/farm if you were successful. Nowadays with the invasion of the new crofters bringing legislation and litigation, all the fun has gone. Sheep acting like lawnmowers left nowhere for the hares to hide until now with the set-aside; someone has introduced a few pairs which are holding their own. Rabbits never flourished here due to the heavy, thin soil and nowadays there seem to be fewer birds on the shore and on the lochs.

§§§§§

As a young man, I was attracted to bullfighting and as we went to Spain quite often on holiday, I became rather knowledgeable about the business. One night in Barcelona, the matador messed up the kill, hit the pulmonary artery, and the bull walked away from him across the ring vomiting blood with every stride. The bull refused to charge and died alone on the far side of the ring. The matador fled before a barrage of boos and flung cushions. I stood up and walked into the clear Spanish night. There was a fireworks display which I watched with no feeling, apart from that of emptiness, and caught the bus back to the hotel.

    I seemed to lose interest in guns, but the next winter I went out and shot a mallard duck. He looked so sad when I waded out to get him lying in the water. The glorious blue-green of his neck still shone although the eyes soon glazed. On my way home I felt sad and thought that's the last; but I still hung, plucked, cooked and ate it. It did not taste good. My cooking? My conscience? Or maybe my age making me more appreciative of life.

THE BALLACHULISH EXPRESS

The service started in 1903 and was closed by 'kick-in-the-pants' Beeching in 1966. It was supposed to connect with the Mallaig line at Fort William, but ended at Ballachulish, because of:

1. shortage of funds, and
2. opposition from the quarry as the required bridge at Ballachulish would hinder shipping.

The train stopped at Connel Ferry, North Connel, Benderloch, Barcaldine Halt, Creagan, Appin, Duror, Kentallen, Ferry Halt, Ballachulish and took about an hour and a half. Its history:

1896 West Highland Railway Ballachulish Extension Act passed
1903 Opened by Stewarts of Ballachulish
1966 Closed

Cars and buses took over, and we became more reserved, although to this day if there are four passengers on an English bus, they sit in separate corners, and in our Ballachulish bus, they will all cram into the same seat to get the *craic*[1].

The children going to Oban High School were much in evidence, but it was as the nights drew in and at weekends, that the *hòro-gheallaidh*[2] set in. As the train left Oban, you could hear the bangs of the lightbulbs as they were removed and thrown out of the windows to facilitate more intimate courting. This rose to the name being given of the Conception Express.

This train was a no-corridor job (not handy for being able to leave at any time) with windows that opened with a leather belt, and a luggage rack that was so substantial that you could sleep in it, and some actually did. It had

---

[1] fun, good time
[2] cavorting

plush cushions which raised clouds of dust when you hit them and views of Mallaig and Kinlochleven decorated the walls.

After competing at the 1957 Oban Games and winning coconuts at the Shows (The Fair), a chum and I were escorting a pair of young ladies home to Lismore. We had only recently made their acquaintance, and were on our best behaviour: hair combed, teeth brushed, and with 'we guys to be trusted' written across our fizzogs. Besides the girls, our compartment companions on the other side of the carriage were three young men. None of them spoke. It was difficult to carry out a meaningful conversation with the ladies with this backdrop.

§§§§§

There were coal deposits along the train route. This was not for taking aboard but because of slinging it off for the rellies who collected it later at their convenience. The Ballachulish Express used more coal than the *Flying Scotsman*.

'She's awfy greedy on coal.'

'Aye, the biler's past its best.'

This was partly true, as she laboured, shuddered and wheezed up the hill out of Oban. A bit out of the town, there's a long bend in the track and over the years, as progress slowed and the boiler steam was reduced, she slowed to a stiff walk, allowing the firemen to jump off, shoot a couple of rabbits and join the train again at the end of the curve.

For twenty years or so, a burly conductor kept a semblance of order on the train. When things got truly out of hand and the communication cord was pulled, they stopped the train and the conductor got off, walked up to the offending carriage and thrashed the happy bunny that had a coil of cord in his hand! If the offender was a budding politician or banker and had dumped the cord, the conductor hammered the lot of them in that carriage. He then walked slowly back to the engine and, with a nod to the driver, the express continued on its merry way.

Times change, the automobile became the freedom way to travel and we became more self-sufficient, isolated, self-centred and selfish; Margaret Thatcher must be very happy!

My father's people came to Lismore from the Glencoe/Ballachulish area and I suppose I regard that as my spiritual home; I know my father did. For some reason, we often made derogatory gags about Ballachulish; before it had a wash and brush up in the 1960s, it was not a very attractive village, with its piles of grey slate.

Many years ago, two friends and I were coming home after a hard ~~drinking~~ sailing week in the Utter Hebrides and stopped at Craignure for sustenance. We had fallen out and were not speaking much. I was puce green from a following sea, Neil's forehead was stitched and one eye closed from a rugby clash with a concrete post and Donald was weary and wearing (I kid you not) full Hieland dress. As we silently left the pub after a blast of the 'electric soup', one *bodach*[3] said to his knowledgeable mate:

'Cò às a tha iad?' (Where are they from?)

'Buinidh iad do Bhail' a' Chaolais!' (They must be from Ballachulish) was the reply.

Enough said!

---

[3] old man

THE BALLACHULISH BRIDGE

Jim and I stocked up in Oban. The method of loading the lager cans was to drop them one at a time into the rubber boat. It was low water springs at 1 a.m. so one in three cans bounced out of the Avon. We abandoned this method and climbed down a shaky ladder in the darkness with the carrier bags in the teeth! The fishing fleet was due in at 2 a.m. and having been witness to an 80-foot fishing boat crushing a fragile trimaran the year before, we hastily left. The skipper of the fishing boat was reputed to have said, 'Ach, they're funny-looking bloody things anyway.'

We motored around to Dunstaffnage. As dawn was breaking, Jim decided to play the fiddle. He played it in the cabin, the cockpit, on deck and in the rubber boat. Dunstaffnage people still speak about the early morning fiddler and 'The Hen's March to the Midden', by now a famous fiddle tune.

Teatime found us under sail, approaching the newly-erected Ballachulish Bridge. I had no idea what clearance we would have, but assumed a Hurley 22 would be OK. A full flood was running and suddenly Jim shouted, 'We're going to hit!'

9 The Ballachulish Bridge

I have no idea if the mistake in the 50-foot clearance was to do with the new specs or the lager consumption. I spun the boat around and started the Seagull. The wind was down the loch, so now we were under sail with the engine at full throttle and doing four knots. But the flood was running at five knots. Slowly and gracefully we went under the bridge in reverse. I just held on—as one does. After tying up at Bishop's Bay and seeking sustenance and succour in the pub, I was chatting to an old Oban school friend,

'Ye'll no believe this Lachie,' says he, 'but not half an hour ago, some mad b*****d went under the bridge backwards.'

'Some bloody tourist,' says I, with a shake of the head (word travels fast on the West Coast).

'Aye,' says he turning back to his pint, 'they're thick on the ground just now.'

REFLECTIONS ON THE GAMES

I had been telling people that it was thirty years since I had been to The Games, and then realised it was forty. Why do I go old on the outside but feel twenty-five in my head? When I was wee, it seemed that all of Lismore went to The Games, leaving a *bodach*[1] and *cailleach*[2] and a few sheepdogs to hold the fort. By the 2000s, apart from a few old warriors like Donald and Archie, no-one seemed to bother. It used to be a Thursday and the children got the day off. Now they don't and it's earlier in the year for the tourists.

The march through the town still takes place with the Oban Pipe Band in the vanguard, led by a pipe major and his amazing silver-mounted baton. One year he threw it up so high it stuck in the telephone wires! We spoke about that in Lismore for weeks. Mind you, in the days before television, three gags had to last us all winter. Then came the gentry with their kilts and eagle feathers, their Bo-Peep *cromagan*[3], and enough heather to hide an SAS squad. Why is it with these people that the women look lovely and a lot of the men look as though they've been let out for the weekend? The proletariat came last, but there were lots of them.

There was an excitement about going in through the turnstiles and seeing the tents and flags, which always had a mediaeval air. There was always a piper playing somewhere, or one tuning up behind the toilets. The girls pranced all day in kilt, doublet and hose, copying dances of martial men who had put the fear of God into their forefathers. Big men throwing stones and hammers in a methodical, purposeful manner, men imposing their will on dogs who, in turn, hypnotised sheep and ducks. Would he make the dog do

---

[1] old man
[2] old woman
[3] crooks

the sword dance? Did the SSPCA know about this? Would the animal rights people sabotage The Games? It might liven things up.

The runners heard the crack of a pistol and the half-mile had started. A big muscular man was in the lead, but you knew that the floater on his shoulder would pass him, pitter-patter, pitter-patter, in the straight. Running middle-distance at high school and university was one thing, but here the hardmen ruled, especially in the tight bends of a 220-yard track; no prisoners taken and no quarter given. After all these years the breathing and the heartbeat quickens, there are butterflies in the stomach and the adrenaline flows again. Silly old fool, you'll give yourself a heart attack.

I asked the ice-cream man for a 99, thought of a good gag, looked at his face and decided 'forget it'. The rain started, my spirits fell and I walked to the boat. May be I'd grown too old for The Games, or perhaps they are from an older, kinder age.

HARD WORK, LISMORE PIER

The four-letter words that are going out of fashion: HARD WORK

When I finished high school, they had started to tart up Lismore pier which had originally been built in 1886. The outfit always employed local labour, but I was the only one to apply for a job. Being under the age of 18, the foreman said that I could be the tea boy, and I in my modest way said 'no'; I could shovel with the best.

'Right,' he said, 'jump up on that wagon and load aggregate at Point.' This was the jetty at the north end of the island, approximately five and half miles from Achnacroish. When we reached there, I stepped in with a will, sending streams of gravel into the truck until an old hand said, 'Stop it, Lachie. He will expect us to do that all the time!' I had a lot to learn about the game, but at least I received full wages.

The weather was good, the *craic* was great and I had a real man's job. I was drinking whisky and courting girls. Some guy, eh?

The project, which was to have lasted three months, lasted most of the year, and had three engineers and three foremen. My favourite gaffer was a Mr Mac from the Utter Hebrides, who, on arrival, climbed up on the lorry and addressed us from on high.

'Boys, I always arrive on a job drunk and leave the same way.'

I liked the guy's style and thought that this is going to be a good summer, threw my hat in the air and shouted 'Hooray!'

I was making almost £20 a week and gave half of it to my mother. God bless my mother; when I failed my first year at university and had no grant to repeat the year, she gave me my wages back for my fees. She had kept it in a separate account, just in case! To keep myself, I tutored school kids and sold Kleeneze Brushes door-to-door, at which I was not a big success, but developed some muscle carrying my suitcase around.

After the buzz of 1945, Lismore had been asleep for years, a sort of heuchtar-teuchtar Brigadoon, and the burst of new faces and bodies awakened lots of deep feelings; romances sprang forth like long dormant buds and the air throbbed with drink and passion.

But to return to hard work. Because we were building a new pier, we needed a diver. He was a professional used to working with professionals and not amateurs like me. The gaffer picked on me, knowing I was on my way to university and thought I must be smart. He shouted a stream of instructions, punctuated by advanced profanity and then the diver went over the side. I panicked, spun various dials on the air machine, and the diver soon appeared

10 Lismore Pier, 1950s—after I fixed it!

back on the surface, looking like the Michelin Man, his suit well-rounded and he not a happy puppy. He soon left, reflecting loudly on our parentage, and the company had to teach a joiner from South Uist to do the job. He was the only one who fitted the suit; health and safety—*mo thòn*[1]! He and I were given a day to get our act together.

The mechanic I worked with, a lovely man called Fergie, got so fed up with me losing tools that he would only give me one if I tied it around my

---

[1] my backside!

neck with a rope. We gave him a going away party when he left, which coincided with the local dance on the island, which was wilder and better-fuelled than usual. The pier working mob was looked upon as competition by the other young men of the island. I was a sort of piggy in the middle, having a foot in both camps.

A huge, friendly labourer with muscles like Charles Atlas and a brain the size of a pea, in a moment of hilarity, tried to dance with me. I don't think he had a hinge in his kilt but he was trying to be friendly—too friendly—and in a fit of exasperation I shoved this gentle giant in the chest. He staggered back on his heels as only a drunk can do and disappeared into a forest of stacked chairs. He reappeared with his eyes flashing death, and I made off through the women's cloakroom; discretion being the better part of valour. Some clown had locked the exit; me and my university career were only saved by the timely arrival of the foreman.

The following morning we appeared for work in such a state that big Mac (the kettle calling the pot black) said to us, 'You can't be here in this state when the Oban boat comes. Go to Point and load the wagon.'

Bad move; within half an hour, we had a 'cargo' over on the Appin Ferry and the party started again. At midday, Mrs Point (on the island we always called folk by the name of their croft or house) called, saying, 'Come quickly, World War III has broken out.'

Some men were fighting, some were swimming with their clothes on, some were wandering about like lost souls; yours truly was found asleep in the wagon on top of the load. Big Mac appeared, climbed on top of the wagon (he loved the big occasion), fired us all and said we were a disgrace to Gaeldom and the human race. On Monday at 8 p.m. he hired us all back again.

For a while, we had an ex-army engineer, complete with his own batman. This engineer was resplendent in the blazer and tie, but even on the hottest day he wore a Mackintosh. He slipped on wet stones one day and all was revealed; there was no *tòn* to his trousers. Even on a good salary, two or three bottles of gin a day (his good lady liked a small refreshment as well) fairly eats into the wages.

We had our tea in the pier shed on wet days, and I had speedily graduated to advanced swearing and boasting in an effort to keep up with my workmates. One day as I was holding court, my back to the shed door, the audience fell silent and I turned around to find my father standing in the door, dressed for the bad weather, oilskins, boots, and sou'wester. He looked at me, shook his head sadly and walked away. He never mentioned it, but I felt about six inches high. My father was a small man, but with a big presence, as befits the skipper of one of ICI's dynamite boats; you needed more than bravado to captain these ships.

When it came time to go to university, my father saw me off. 'Well Lachlan, I hope you're successful in your chosen profession but, for the life of me, why you are going up to university to study for five years to become a dentist is beyond my comprehension. A teacher, a doctor or even a minister, I could understand.'

Of course, he was right then, and now, in 2019, with the shortage of NHS dentists in the UK, it will be cut down to two years at the local tech college, and then let loose on the public's molars. My father used to say that when you got your ticket as a master mariner, you made most of your mistakes in the first three years. I qualified in January 1966 and practised in England until 1970.

UNIVERSITY YEARS

I was so astonished to get my Higher Leaving Certificate when I left school that I went into a state of shock for weeks.

My brother-in-law Robin gave me a book called *Your Future,* which covered everything in alphabetical order from Actors to Zebra Farming. By the time I got to the Ds, I had run out of time. You see, I had a date with an angel to see *Love is a Many-Splendored Thing* at the flicks in Stranraer that night. 'I want to be a dentist,' I shouted over my shoulder as I ran for the bus. Two minutes either way and I could have been a dancer or a doctor.

I had nothing against dentists, as the local Stranraer one had saved my teeth; the one in Oban used to pull them out and give me a shilling for being a good boy. No, not *that;* mother was always with me!

At the university interview for dentistry, they asked me why I had picked Queen's College, Dundee (then part of St Andrews University). I had been brought up to tell the truth, so I said, 'it was the only one with a vacancy.' I was a marked man from day one.

I had been doing good times in my sixth-year high school for the 880-yards but, to my eternal regret, I abandoned sport for drink, women and eightsome reels (rock and roll).

For my first year in university, I stayed in the Airlie Residential Hall in Dundee until I was asked to leave for a variety of reasons. The copper wire in the fuse box finally sealed my fate. I stayed in the annexe, which gave me more freedom than most; you could smuggle girls up the back stairs if you avoided the housemaster. I found the rule that on Sunday afternoon you could take girls to your room for a game of Scrabble or whatever and then down in the evening for high tea—a little bizarre. I, of course, had produced my partner after the first year ball for her breakfast; she was still in her ball gown—shock, horror!

The other Scottish universities at this time were 90% Scots. At St Andrews we had Africans, Arabs, English, Norwegians, and that was great, exciting and educational. This was university before the politicians pumped the young into tertiary education because there were no real jobs for them, the system for producing artisans having collapsed. We were soon to be on the road of PhDs in Yoghurt-tasting from Clachnacuddin University.

Some of the students at Queen's College, Dundee wore red gowns, as did the rest of the St Andrews' students across the river, but not us, the boys of the QCD! We were too cool (yes, we used that word then, too). We wore tight trousers and winkle-pickers—at least I did. Oh yes, when seen from a distance, the red gowns were colourful and the way they wore them interesting: first year properly on both shoulders, second year off one shoulder, third year off two shoulders, final year dragging from around the elbows with a very dusty hem to show how senior they were to the Bejants[1]. The ultimate, of course, was the postgraduate, who dragged theirs down the street on the end of a rope!

I was not quite as sophisticated as I pretended to be, and one evening I went out for a meal with some of the new English boys I had just met. I was banging on about something as usual, when the waitress asked which dessert I would like. I gave a cursory glance at the menu and said, 'Yorkshire pudding.'

'Yorkshire pudding?' she repeated, with a raised eyebrow, and knowing I had put my foot in it somehow, I said breezily, 'Yes, and lots of custard.' I ate the lot with apparent relish, and one of my new English friends said tentatively, 'We usually have Yorkshire pudding with roast beef down South.' 'Never,' said I, with great aplomb. 'The Scots always eat it with custard.'

The Student Union dances were good, but the Empress Ballroom had the best jazz bands. We had a childish competition for free beer as to who could find and dance with the girl with the best legs, best face, the best figure and so on. On this particular night, it was the ugliest girl in the ballroom. I won hands down. Unfortunately, this turned out to be a huge man—in a dress. I had reached university without knowing about homosexuals or transvestites; there were not many obvious ones back on the croft in these days, let alone a stevedore in a frock. He kept a good grip of me in the dance hall, promising me untold delights later in Lochee[2], but I broke free and escaped up the Perth Road with 'come back here, ye wee Hielan' hoor' ringing in my ears.

---

[1] freshers, first years
[2] reputedly tough area of Dundee

The jute mills were still operational in Dundee, and it was an amazing sight to see the gates open at *lowsin-time*[3], and an avalanche of girls and women in curlers, the older with metal versions and the younger with pink plastic rollers and huge *jabbie-thrus*[4] to keep them in place, all wearing wraparound flowery *peenies*[5], short skirts and *baffies*[6] pour forth. The husbands, the *kettle-bilers*[7], were often unemployed and at home, so there was emancipation in Dundee two generations before it arrived for the rest of us. The fact that the girl you walked home from the dance on a Friday night asked you out on Saturday did not mean that she was easy.

§§§§

My lack of academic study, my fast mouth and innate sense of fairness, which is built into most young people, got me into a lot of hot water in those days. I have always hated favouritism, and to prove a point, we presented the same job to the same professor three times in one afternoon. He gave one pal three out of five, another, his favourite, he gave four out of five and the last, the one he seemed to dislike, he told him it was rubbish and to do it again. Point made, but did I keep my mouth shut about this? Did I hell! I could talk myself into so much trouble.

Another example: I am in the lab, at the start of third year, telling the lab technicians tales from the croft, when a new, wee guy walks in wearing a lab coat much too big for him. Slapping him on the shoulder, I say welcomingly, 'You'll like working with the boys here, there a good boozy bunch with a great selection of dirty jokes.'

And I exit into the lecture theatre.

Two minutes later, the wee guy turns up, walks to the podium and starts his lecture. He looks directly at me with a seriously disgruntled face, and I curl up and die.

§§§§

[3] end of workday or shift
[4] small plastic sticks through the rollers
[5] pinafores
[6] slippers
[7] house-husband (pejorative)

The problem with studying is you need a lot of books, often very big, long books. I hated big text books and found a nice, thin, Yankee book on oral surgery and took it to the Prof's lecture to see if it would be adequate to cover my needs. Now in those days this prof was a god and his lectures were looked upon as something approaching The Sermon on the Mount. Totally engrossed in checking the Yankee textbook against the Prof's own (which was the big thick one) and checking both with what he was saying, I finally realised more from the breath being held around me that there was a voice saying somewhere, 'MacDonald, what are you doing?' Panic sets in, and I realise all eyes are on me; I get it all round the wrong way and blurt out, 'I am just checking to see if your lecture is adequate, Sir.' Gasps of horror around me bring it home to me what I have just done; he now knows I'm barking mad. I may never pass this course.

§§§§§

The five years rolled by, and many a night I rolled home from the Queen's Hotel in Perth Road. I was becoming more disillusioned with everyone, including myself. There were some who did much to help me on my way: a good man, HC, who taught me how to extract teeth and called a spade a spade; a Prof Mac who taught me how to deal with kids in pain; and even a Prof of False Teeth, who threw me out of his clinic on a regular basis for insolence, but who, I believe, pushed me through my finals, because he liked people who stood up to him. Most of all, I was grateful to the semi-retired, modest general practitioners who came in to correct your work with words of encouragement and, of course, those who caused us amusement like the Prof who used to rescue you from badly snapped off roots and who would always say to the theatre nurse, in a good, strong Yorkshire accent, '(h)aaand me ma root forceps, lass; I'm goin' in after 'em.'

There were more normal people outside of the hospital, but as usual, I was sailing pretty close to the wind, and if it were not for my wife and daughter, I don't think I would ever have qualified.

Diane and I got married before I qualified and then Seònaid came along. We rented a two-roomed tenement flat for 15 shillings a week, with air-raid shelters out the back and a shared loo on the circular staircase. There was a massive pole in the back green with pulleys running to each flattie/balcony to dry your clothes. When everyone had their coal fires on and the wind in the west, the nappies came in a sooty brown. We made it into a cosy wee flat when Diane got a job, risking life and limb, working in a List D school. Both sets of parents helped out and at weekends up in Forfar we ate ourselves to a standstill and got through the rest of the week on potatoes and bread. Di could do marvellous things with spuds, but my favourite dish was an Irish mixed grill: boiled potatoes, fried potatoes and chips!

Eventually, they gave me a small white piece of paper which said BDS (passed at last), and let me loose on the general public. Unfortunately, I remained a student in my head for another 17 years, until I eventually saw the light. What a privilege it was to have the chance to go to university, and what a shame it took me so long to realise and appreciate the fact.

ARMY DAYS

I had one three-week holiday in Germany at the expense of the British Army, which was not a total success. I did not have the correct attitude for a career army officer in Her Majesty's Forces.

In the early 1960s, the British Army was short of doctors and dentists, and if you were accepted, you were taken on in fifth year as a second lieutenant and, when qualified, made a captain. My meagre grant was not keeping pace with my lifestyle, so I filled in papers in Dundee, was interviewed and accepted as a possible officer and gentleman, with a three-week trial run in Germany. I have since discovered that our family is related to Major General Sir Hector Archibald MacDonald of the Sudan, but maybe we'll draw a veil over that one.

They are nice, polite people, the British Army officers, but as always, the majority are middle-class English and the grunts are Northern English from poor suburban areas, or Scottish. There were a dozen or so of us, mainly English boys, with three Celts: myself, a chap from Belfast and a Welshman—honest. They flew us over in a transport carrier, belted into bucket seats, flying—it appeared to me—20 feet above a stormy North Sea. First time in a plane at twenty-three I appeared cool, but was keeping a tight grip on all sphincters. The chap in charge was a major—an army dentist—a lovely man who had to look after this bunch of lunatics.

I checked out the mob and reckoned that I could handle most of them, either mentally or physically, except the big Irish guy. After a few drinks in the mess that night, I challenged him to a drinking contest and then a fight. Later on that night I picked up two second prizes! Pecking order established, we got on fine.

They moved us every two or three days to a new medical camp; Osnabrück, Dortmund, Hanover and eventually a long weekend in West Berlin.

One dental surgery is the same as the next, so we had a lot of time on our hands. Long wet lunches, a siesta to recover and then down to dinner. This was boring, as we were advised not to discuss religion, politics or sex, thus leaving me virtually speechless. I discovered that I could not do small talk, having been brought up in a family where the one that spoke the loudest won the day. Father blamed his loud voice on a lifetime of shouting orders from an open bridge, so I guess the rest of us followed suit.

Fortunately, the women officers—captains were nursing sisters and lieutenants were staff nurses—had an open invite to their quarters after dinner for drinkie-poos. Most of the male officers were accompanied by their wives, who watched them like hawks; the girls were not encouraged to court civilians or non-comms[1]—and then we arrived. It was Christmas every day.

The old gag of 'officers and their ladies, sergeants and their wives, and other ranks and their women' kept running in my head, but I kept my mouth shut when sober, which was not often, as the CO[2] often picked up our bar bill, but even if you had to pay for it, it was sixpence[3] a glass.

I discovered early on that they were treating us like real officers, and that if I rang a bell a chap in a white coat appeared.

'A large whisky and chaser, please.'

'Certainly, Sir. Will that be all?'

Magic.

Another bad move was that the Irishman and I discovered that instead of hanging about after dinner talking inconsequential crap to each other, a good idea was to adjourn to the sergeants' mess where the real action was. Officers don't do that sort of thing.

We convinced a sergeant with whom we had been drinking all night to take us to the firing range in the early morning. Armed with a couple of Brens, all was going swimmingly well until some idiot blew away a tomcat that was on its way home after a night on the tiles. The sergeant took a dim view of this, threw us into the back of the truck and dumped us back at the barracks.

I tended to wander off on my own, and on one occasion jumped into a taxi in the early morning, mumbled 'Army Camp' and he took me to the

---

[1] non-commissioned officers
[2] commanding officer
[3] equivalent to 2½ new pence (present day).

American army camp. A nice, big American drove me back to ours as we sang Paul Robson songs to while away the time.

It was Berlin where the *cac*[4] really hit the fan. The Berlin wall had only been up a couple of years and the first night there I fell asleep on the S-train which goes into East Berlin and woke up surrounded by Russians and East German guards asking me questions. Having only English and Gaelic, I was unable to communicate with them, but showed them my passport and passes, and the Brits sent a jeep over for me. Oh boy, I had visions of the Gulag and the salt mines, but no-one was laughing on the way back.

The strip joints in Berlin were OK, if you sat at the bar; if you sat at the tables, the girls came over and ordered cheap Babycham at enormous prices. We of course found a really cheap joint where the floor show consisted of four well-built middle-aged *fräus* who emerged one at a time through bead curtains and marched about a postage-stamp stage, stark-naked, to music from a *Wurlitzer*. We were thrown out!

Towards the end of the tour, we sat with a squad of subalterns (real sodjers) listening to some top brass lunatic who apparently was looking forward to fighting the Ruskies. I had been rudely awakened from my post-luncheon nap and was tired and confused, as they often are down in Westminster.

'Any questions?' (This was a rhetorical question.)

'Sir, if a Russian paratrooper comes crashing through my surgery window, am I supposed to fight him?' (Smart-assed MacDonald.)

'Certainly.' (Maybe he thought I was a real soldier.)

'Don't be ridiculous!' (Or words to that effect.)

The major got a hold of me later.

'Fancy a drink, Lachlan?'

'Are you serious about joining the Army, Lachlan?'

'Don't think I'm cut out for it, Sir.'

'Probably right, Lachlan, probably right.'

You have to admit their manners are excellent. I returned home and went to bed for a few days.

'An robh thu trang anns a' Ghearmailt, Lachuinn?' (Were you busy over in Germany, Lachlan?)

'Bha, a Mhàthair. Uarraidh.' (Yes, Mother. Very.)

---

[4] excrement

HARD WORK: LOCH AWE

I had badly broken my right arm and then failed my finals, so I found a job at Loch Awe to:
1. earn money to re-sit my finals and feed my family;
2. give my arm a severe testing to ensure that it would stand up to dentistry (crazy, eh?).

The Loch Awe Hydro scheme was the last one in Scotland and was unique in that the dam was halfway up Ben Cruachan and could be refilled at night from Loch Awe by reversible turbines. The turbines kick in when a lot of electricity is needed in the National Grid fast, so the shafts from the dam to the turbines are massive.

Calum and I lined up at 7.30 a.m. in front of the GF[1], he seemed to know a lot of people really well,

'McGinty, you're trouble; on your way.'

'McLeod, you can't get out of your bed on Mondays; off you go.'

'Who are you?' We did look a bit different.

'We're the students.' (in chorus)

'I don't hire students. They're a f***ing waste of time. But somebody did speak up for you [Calum's uncle]. I'll start you, but you won't last a week.'

'B***er you!' I said, *sotto voce*.

'What's that?'

'I'm over the flu.'

[1] general foreman

11 Loch Awe

'What do *you* do?' He addressed Calum. (This could turn into a rap.)
'I'm an art student.'
'OK. You join the cement finishing squad; that's artistic.'
This guy is a comedian. He looked questioningly at me.
'I'm a dental student,' said I.
'I've got the very job for you. Join Willie's lot.' The Jack Hammer Squad!
This guy is a cruel comedian. I had used pneumatic drills before at the Lismore Pier, but nothing as huge and heavy as these things. I had a problem lifting them, never mind bloody using them. I used one all day, and my hands went into spasm, the sinews tightened and stuck as clenched fists. I had to hold my irons[2] in clenched fists to eat my breakfast. This caused huge amusement to my fellow workers, who formed a circle to watch my ham-fisted attempt. When they saw I was not going to jack it in, they accepted me. The Hielanders and the Irish have a long tradition in hydro schemes and if you pulled your weight, for the most part, they were great—with a few exceptions. Like the guy I shared a room[3] with, who seemed OK for a few weeks and then went on the piss; he changed before my eyes into a nasty, evil thing. He started drinking on Thursday, drank solidly until Sunday and then

---

[2] cutlery
[3] two army cots and a chest of drawers

disappeared. Thank goodness; I was sleeping with one eye open, my hand over my throat and my back securely against the wall.

We stayed in the camp a few miles from the tunnel and sang about the company, 'Nuttall, Nuttall, good for f*** all.' Going in on the bus and when the shift changed, the men shouted, 'How's she cutting?' Soft rock was good and hard rock was bad.

We were supplied with bed, board, fags and beer by the company, but all at a high price, there being nowhere else to go. The wages for a 12-hour shift, seven days a week were large but then so was the super—or emergency—tax which came straight out of our pay packets every week. By the time we paid the store for all the rest, there was not a lot of money left. Talk about 'I owe my soul to the Company store'; we had to do something.

Just above the tunnel entrance, below the railway line and beside a small stream, we built a shelter with an old tent and some bits and pieces. One of the guys had been in the army, so we had raised sleeping platforms, a latrine, drainage and so on. It was such a success that we took in lodgers: two painters from Glasgow. This was a bad move. They were mad, bad, keen on women and booze, and had some bad genes. Fortunately for us, one night, both drunk and arguing, they decided to cook over the open fire. The frying pan was huge, heavy and full of hot fat. The more evil of the two lifted it high to smash the other over the head with it. As he flung it backwards, the boiling fat cascaded over his own shoulders. One guy was out cold and the other was screaming and crawling around on the ground. We administered first aid but did not break our backs getting help, and after they left, we never saw them again. I did not lose sleep over our two lodgers.

We worked mostly in the main chamber in the middle of the mountain and it was huge. When the whistle went for *lowsin-time*, we sat to eat our pieces[4]. Thirty feet below, a squad was putting in one of the turbines. A local piper programmed his mate, who fancied himself as a soccer star; rolling up his piece bag into a ball he shouted, *'Heid!'* as he threw it down. One Friday, he threw a fresh egg; naturally he had spread the word that day, and half the workforce came to cheer as the catcher below got egg all over his face.

It was difficult to cook in the tent, and so at night we jumped on a bus or a truck which ran back and forward to the camp all the time. If we could not get a ticket for a main meal (someone was always coming on or off the spree),

---

[4] sandwiches

you could eat as many free soups and puddings as you could keep down. We were a bit starved of meat, and one weekend, I watched in awe as Calum ordered and ate two huge mixed grills; forget the carbs, gies the protein! The weather was not good in the last few weeks of our work in Argyll and the old tent was leaking badly. I bribed an old guy who liked his dram to give us the key to an old Nissan hut. Ach, it was dry and we were young.

§§§§§

The night squad that replaced us drove past in the main tunnel most nights about 1800 hours. Other workers were pouring concrete in one of the main shafts that day, and we were working below them. Half an hour after we left, the whole lot came down and killed or injured half of the squad that replaced us. I managed to phone my parents who were close by in Lismore but my wife was with her parents in Angus. One of her friends from London phoned to tell her how sorry she was to hear about my death at Loch Awe. My wife fainted still holding the telephone. Of course, the papers reported a MacDonald killed, but since we were in the Highlands, most realised there would be more than one of the same clan working here! The phone lines were blocked and it was the following day before my wife got word that I was OK. Safety was not such a priority in 1965.

§§§§§

This taste of hard graft gave me a great boost to get on and qualify. When you are looking down the barrel of a twelve-bore shotgun, it fairly concentrates the mind.

Getting fired was difficult. The gaffer was a decent man, built like a barge, but was not going to win the Brain of Britain competition. He had come to rely on me to remember where things were, like mixers, shovels and jacks. My comrades dropped everything when the whistle went, and it drove me nuts looking for the same things every day. I thought I had the money I was due in lying time worked out for a holiday with my wife and baby daughter before I started back for my final few months at university and then was told it would be weeks before I actually received it. That was no good; I needed it now! Fortunately, a man who knew the score told me, 'You'll have to get the bullet. If you get fired, you'll get it in your hand.'

That Friday I went in late, did everything wrong: lost the dumper keys, dropped bits down the shaft, broke this, broke that—everything but run the ganger down—all to no avail. 'What's wrong with you today, Lachie?' was the worst I could get out of the foreman. Desperation, and then I thought of it: he hated drink and had sacked men on suspicion. So I went off, quite eagerly, to the nearest pub, the Tight Line, had a few *haufs*, went back down the tunnel weaving and singing a Gaelic song and as expected, he went mental! 'Get tae th' office and get yer f***ing books,' he yelled at me. 'You good for nothin' Teuchter!' Success! I was off like a shot.

Some years later, now qualified and back in Scotland, I met my old gaffer in a café. We swapped stories and I was going to tell him this story when he said, 'Do you remember the day I sacked you, Lachie?' I nodded at him. 'I'm sorry, but you gave me no option. Maybe it was for the best, because you're now a real dentist with your own family and practice.' I was so glad I kept my mouth firmly shut!

That life was OK for a few short months when you're young, but I take my hat off to the Tunnel Tigers, who did it for Scotland for over half a century—a difficult job.

12 Entrance to Cruachan Power Station, Loch Awe

DENTISTRY I

When I graduated in 1966, I had been at university so long that some people thought I was a member of staff; thus I can go to two different class reunions.

Mother and Father were getting old, so I applied for a job in Edinburgh. I was whisked off in a limo to a mansion where I was interrogated by the Edinburgh dental mafia. Intuitively I knew I was in danger, and all the signals were flashing red. Having ascertained that I knew nothing about real dentistry, I was fed whisky and then the dental hoods led me into the drawing-room where a vision of pure sexuality lay draped upon a chaise longue, dressed in a slinky, tightly-fitting, one-piece jumpsuit and stroking a white Persian cat which lay on her bosom. I stood awkwardly, polishing my shoe on the back of my trouser leg with my brand new degree clasped in a sweaty hand, answering questions from the goddess as my interrogators eyed me closely.

'What a lovely name. And are you married, Lachlan?'

13 Lachlan B MacDonald, BDS
(the butter would not melt in my mouth!)

'Yes,' I piped a high-pitched affirmative.
'Do you have children?'
'Yes. A daughter.' (Cleared throat.)
'How lovely. I have nothing but my little pussy.'

Oh God, I was going to die. Why had I ever left the croft? The sweat dripped down into the three-piece blue suit, rescued from the pawnshop only yesterday. I fled into the Edinburgh night.

I phoned a lecturer to tell him my sorry tale. He knew the people involved and gave me some good advice:

'I heard you had a job offer in England,' he said.
'Yes, and the ticket,' said I.
'Use it!'

Down South in Coventry, I worked for six months for a man with an unusual name. He was an ex-guardsman and barking mad. The free flat was costly, and although I kept 50% of my fees, I had to pay my own laboratory mechanic—talk about heather growing out of my ears!

I had been used to one patient an hour in the Dental Hospital; my new boss had booked in 30 patients and from the first day, I was a lot more frightened than the patients. Totally losing it one day, I told my boss, in broken Gaelic and English, that I was leaving at the end of the month. Cooling down, I realised that this was Wednesday and the end of the month was the Friday fast approaching that week. The flat went with the job, my wife was six months pregnant, and we already had a toddler and no money.

'That's another fine mess you've got us into!' I could hear her say!

Phoning around, I found a job in Corby, better known in England as 'Little Scotland'. My new boss was called Jack. He was Greenock born and bred, built like a brick outhouse and took no prisoners. He taught me some important points in dentistry which I have never forgotten:

1. don't criticise other people's work, as you usually see their failures
2. don't read tomorrow's day book; there's nothing you can do until they are in the chair
3. the waiting room will be full when we are dead and gone.

He was great; we did everything in that surgery ourselves with no need to refer to a dental hospital which was hours away. After fighting with an impacted wisdom tooth for a while, both dentist and patient in a lather of sweat, I'd ask Jack for help.

'For goodness' sake [well, not quite as polite as that]. Didn't they teach anything at that hospital?'

He would be straight in there with a Couplands[1], and—ping—a second later, the tooth would come flying out through the air. As Jack left my surgery, he would growl at the patient, 'I hope you are not giving Mr Mac any trouble!' Then I would sew the patient's mouth up and get all the applause; he was a class act was Jack.

In Corby, the surgery overlooked the Market Square, where real markets were held once a week. One day, taking an upper impression, I glanced out the window and my attention was held by an attractive young woman. I followed her undulating progress—poetry in motion—across the Market Square. An atmosphere of being watched made me glance down at my patient. Instead of feeling under the upper lip to see if the alginate had set, in my reverie I had my finger up her nose! I could see the headlines in the *News of the World*:

NEW Shock Horror: Pervy Dentist struck off!
No woman safe in Corby!
Dental NHS in crisis!

I laughed, not knowing what else to do, and thank goodness, she did too!

§§§§§

My children were almost two and four years old when the discovery of Scottish oil broke in the news. It was time to go home, get rich and become a citizen rather than a subject. So I found another dental post in Fife, with a chap I knew called Jimmie, another real gent and an old-fashioned socialist to boot. I think of socialists as people who rebel and storm railway stations and so forth. Nowadays, socialists buy a train ticket and write a PhD about storming and rebelling. Fife was jumping in the 1970s and a happening place; life was good there.

Later on, this practice set up in Abu Dhabi but I went to a smart area in Glasgow to set up a practice from scratch in a little-used cul-de-sac in an area awash with dentists. Call me 'Businessman of the Year!'

Soon I was working two jobs—one NHS and one private—and keeping myself going—just and no more. Something had to give—me—but fortunately this was sorted out with a lot of help from family and friends.

---

[1] a type of tooth-removing instrument

I applied for another post at the Gorbals Health Centre, and landed up thinking that I really couldn't take on any more work, but since I had taken the day off for the interview, I went anyway.

Up until now, my dental interviews were held in a gentleman-like manner; we went out to dinner, got drunk and discussed the horrors of general practice. This was different. Here sat a lot of people, few of them dentists, doing what they do best: holding meetings, talking about audits and interviewing people instead of working. When caught on the back foot, I either clam up or go in with the *heid doon*. Focussing on the dental officer in charge of the committee, and ignoring the non-dentists, I went in for a Royal Command Performance: 'Well, well, *a bhalaich*[2],' I said, 'if I had known it was to be a ceilidh, I would have worn the kilt.' (I didn't really need this job anyway.) I launched into a lyrical tale of dental days in Fife and recited a poem I had made up for my colleagues now in Abu Dhabi. This was just after the Scottish soccer team was hammered in Argentina (this Rasta style came twenty years before Ali G).

The Abu Dhabi Infirmary Blues
(with apologies, and to the tune of 'Saint James' Infirmary Blues')

I was walkin' downtown Abu Dhabi
Just smokin' a reefer or two,
When along came the Sheik of the Kingdom
And says, 'Come here you old Dentist, you;
I've been watchin' yo' form for some time now
The success is goin' straight to yo' head,
If you don't kick the booze and the wimmen
Yo' gonna land up stone dead.'
The Dentist said: 'Cool it now, Abdul
Ah can tell when you blowin' yo' fuse
The Fifers are certain of winning
Like Ally's army, we just cannae lose!'
But he ended downtown in the jailhouse,

---

[2] boy (in this context, 'son' or '*ma man*')

Like the cowboys, he died in his shoes.
While the girls in the Cat House keep humming,
The Abu Dhabi Infirmary Blues.

So, with that entertainment, I added, 'Gentlemen, thank you for your attention; you have others waiting.' Then I took off. The following day I received a letter saying that I had been given the job!

Seventeen years later, going up in the lift for my retirement party, I said to the chief dental officer who had been present at that interview, 'It has always puzzled me. Why did I get this job 17 years ago?'

'We thought you would be the best man for the Gorbals, Lachie.'

Unfortunately, I think I know what he meant!

They gave me early retirement, due to a heart attack, but after I did up a boat, worked on the family home, and went round the world to see the rellies, I went into a decline and the Black Dog—depression—set in on me. To the relief of my wife, I went back to work part-time and did my best to hold the NHS together for a bit longer, or like John Henry, the railroad man, 'He died with the hammer (air-rotor) in his hand, Lord, Lord.'

Over the years, I have been involved in the FDC[3], the LHC[4], the LDC[5], the HaHP[6], but I don't last long as I get impatient when things don't happen quickly and I prefer working at the 'enamel face' where I can achieve results in days, weeks or months. I have been involved in the Health Workers' group, the 'Sick Dentist' scheme for many years. I came into the AA Fellowship in 1983 and have stayed there ever since. It's great to see people and families getting their lives together again, and we in dentistry have been fortunate in having sensible, forward-looking people within the General Dental Council to support us.

With my Celtic temperament, dentistry has suited me just fine, and as an old soldier said to me once, 'Lachlan, if you want to *take* a position (as in battle), use a Highland regiment; if you want to *hold* a position, use a Welsh one.' So, like the Highland charge well-known in history, I like to get things done—yesterday—but I get fed-up quickly too!

---

[3] Fife Dental Committee
[4] Local Health Committe
[5] Local Dental Committee
[6] Have a Heart, Paisley

I have never made my fortune at dentistry, taught to believe that this profession is for the primary purpose of relieving pain, educating people on how to look after their teeth and keeping a weather eye out for oral cancer. I just never quite got the hang of charging people money, even in my own private practice, which only lasted three years before the NHS called!

Rabbie Burns called it 'thou hell o' a' diseases', and the Gaelic bards knew all about the horrors of toothache:

> *Mìle marbhphaisg ort a dhéudeadh thar gach galair,*
> *Miashlaint ort mar dh'fhàg thu m' eudail de na fearaibh*

> A thousand curses on you, toothache, of all diseases,
> Cess on you, for the state in which you have left my most cherished of men[7]

Dentistry

(Tune: 'Your Cheatin' Heart', accompanied by a sobbing tenor sax solo)

Your bleedin' gums still make me blue
Ah scale and scale the whole day through
The blood still comes ere what I do
Your bleedin' gums will tell on you.

---

[7] *Achmhasan an Déididh (Curse on the Toothache)*, Tocher volume 22 (1976), page 224. As told by Margaret MacKay (Mairead Dhonnchaidh Chaluim 'ac Aoidh (1872-1963) to Fred Macaualy, for the School of Scottish Studies Archive, University of Edinburgh. Gaelic spelling (unedited), is as appears in *Tocher*.

HAPPY DAYS IN KIRKCALDY

The SNP

'Election results' rearranged reads 'lies, let's recount.'

When I was young, in political terms, we had left, right and centre; now it is all muddled up together and a right old *brochan*[1] too. Labour wanted fair dos for all, Liberals spoke of federalism and went with the flow, and the Tories cried 'discipline' and 'family values'; most of them were sincere. The only sincerity left seems to be a sincere desire to get rich and powerful at any cost.

As fewer and fewer people vote, more and more time is spent by a portion of the media promoting these political creatures. Those of the media whose jobs are involved pay lip-service to these public servants, many of whom have been shown to be liars, cheats and thieves as an increasing chorus from their cohorts in the civil service sing, 'It all makes work for the admin crew to do.'

The ignorance and arrogance of these people is beyond understanding, as can be seen every time they cock-up their e-mails. Even two-bit crooks (as the Americans used to say) know that the only safe way to pass on information is by walking in the park or sitting in the loo with taps running and only then after checking for a wire or a recording device. They obviously have not watched enough American movies.

In the 1970s, when I was doing my PR bit in Kirkcaldy with the SNP, I rattled out letters as 'Lachie MacDonald' which, after all, was my name, but wrote back angry replies to my own letters under the pseudonym of 'James Buchanan', just so that I could liven the debate up a bit. My father's Christian

---

[1] porridge

name was Jimmy and mother's maiden name was Buchanan—it only seemed fair.

I was intrigued by Teddy Taylor, who was MP for Glasgow Cathcart. Teddy was good for a quote 24 hours a day. His platform at that time was family values and capital punishment. My aim was the best politicians of any colour for Scotland, and how naive I was. I wrote to Teddy suggesting that he needed a punchline on which to hang his ideas and that was to bring back public hanging in Cathcart (for a start, it was a dry area) and use the strapline, 'the family that hangs together stays together.' Sadly, I had no reply from Tory headquarters but, after that and several other similar incidents, my home telephone began to click strangely when I picked it up. I lived next door to the secretary of the STUC[2]. His phone was being tapped and since we had a shared line (this was a long time ago), I wondered if 'they' had been party to my Gaelic/English rants.

I believed in personal contact. If I was in the chair it was 20 minutes in the hall and two hours knocking on doors. Mind you, on a winter's night, I was not popular. Where are the politicians in the street banging on the doors these days? Only if the cameras are on them, and then back for a soundbite in the studio. I want to see commitment: punters out on the street spreading the message with a cold North Easterly that would freeze the b***s off a brass monkey, and not sitting on their *tòn* in a hall or gibbering into a telephone.

§§§§§

In the 1970s, when practising my profession on the people of Fife, my wife and I were invited to one of the Queen's Garden Parties. I somehow had the idea that kilts and accessories were out and morning suits were in, but I was 20 years out of date. I turned up at the Palace in full Highland dress as if going to a royal levée. I was armed to the teeth with a dirk and *sgian dubh*[3], hoping that I would be lifted by the cops or at least denied entry, if not thrown out. I could then fill the tabloids with claims of brutality, racism (being a Gaelic-speaking Highlander), at least seeing a return to the Proscription Act and the likelihood of being transported to Botany Bay in

---

[2] Scottish Trades Union Congress. Jimmy Milne and his wife Alice; lovely people. In Jimmy's office all the decor was in red and he had a magnificent array of vodkas from all over the world.

[3] small knife worn as part of Highland dress

chains. Curses! It was not to be. A quarter of the invited punters were in kilts, and no-one paid any attention to me. I cannot remember even seeing the Queen, but ate dinky cucumber sandwiches with George Reid, Iain MacCormick and other like-minded people.

These were exciting times in Fife. The year 1974 was full of elections; there were two. They counted all the votes in Glenrothes Technical College, and in the evening of one of the elections I was dressed in the kilt, and after the booths closed we had a few refreshments. We were very firm about not drinking when in contact with the public! I was in the lavvies having a Jimmy Riddle and made some smart comment to the opposition. A flying picket group who had appeared that day approached me. My companion melted away, and I was saved from a fate worse than death by the timely arrival of those old political warhorses Harry Gourlay and Willie Hamilton.

When Westminster tried to amalgamate Fife and Kinross, the Fifers stood up to a man/woman, and cried, 'B***er off—this is the Kingdom of Fife.' I was so proud of these people that I made myself an honorary Fifer and started using *weel-kent* greetings like, *'Ye hoor, Tam. We'll aye be sailin' oot o' Deysart fishin' the pertains, sir.'* [4]

Of course, when I worked out of the Gorbals Health Clinic for 17 years, I regarded myself as an honorary Gorbalese and then it was, *'Fleet, ya bass, wha'r you starin' at, son?'* [5]

In the 1970s I had a big poster in the front window in Kirkcaldy saying: 'Scotland's Oil Will Make England Great Again.' Two old wifies standing on the pavement with one saying to the other: *'Whit fur dae we want tae mak England Great Again?*

I tore the poster down in disgust.

It does not matter to the Unionists if 80% or 20% of the people vote and as a well-known mayor of London[6] once said, 'If voting changed anything, they'd abolish it.' If you don't vote we'll waken up one day to hear that the people have so much faith in what they are doing that the Government will just suspend the elections for another year or two.

---

[4] You whore, Tam. We'll always be sailing out of Dysart fishing the crabs.
[5] Watch it! What are you looking at?
[6] Ken Livingstone

It's not true that apathy rules. In Edinburgh, the city of the law abiders, someone at a recent election attacked the ballot boxes with a number seven iron. It's not the storming of the Winter Palace or the Bastille, but it's a start.

Nowadays, with many of the decisions taken in Brussels[7] and Westminster, and the Scottish Unionist parties dancing to their London bosses' tunes, if you want to have any say in your country, you vote SNP. It's pretty simple and you know it makes sense.

---

[7] This may change any day now! (2019)

The Happening

The scene is Kirkcaldy, circa 1975, and the event is a prestigious get-together organised by my friend DH, the town artist. *A'body*[1] was in town that day: writers, poets and artists and people who wanted to be writers, poets and artists. I locked onto my daughter's English teacher and after a splendid lunch, we went to take in the show or shows—it truly was a Kirkcaldy Festival. Had it matured, it might have outshone the Edinburgh one!

Our first port of call was the bold Alan, who was reading his verses. Alan had partaken of the Highland brew and when some lasses in the audience moved, he reprimanded them in the most forceful fashion. 'Out of order,' said my friend and I, who swiftly vacated the premises.

The day passed in a haze of cavorting, singing and general good cheer, and I felt a bit like Tam o' Shanter as darkness fell. All was not lost, however, as my friend invited me into the holy of holies, an upstairs venue reserved for the *crème de la crème*.

MacDiarmid, Morgan and Henderson were rubbing shoulders with the best in the land, but tension had been building all day over the place of Scots or *Lallans* in the Scottish art establishment.

I, a complete bystander in those affairs, became a bit bored, as the drink had run out and no-one was paying any attention to me! Leaping to my feet, I proclaimed that where I came from we either spoke Gaelic or English, and I regarded Scots as either a dialect of Anglo-Saxon or as a bastardisation of the Queen's English.

The bold Alan, a supporter of Rabbie, took a race at me, but hit the bloke beside me. All hell broke loose, and going forward to where Mr MacDiarmid sat and shielding him with my coat from the flying glass said, 'How are you keeping?' to which he replied, puffing his pipe, 'The boys are having a fine time tonight.' Me? Exit stage left. My friend visited my wife the following day and told her that I had ruined the whole show and had put the kibosh on the budding Kirkcaldy Festival.

From then on I was known as AMF: all my fault.

---

[1] everyone

DENTISTRY II
GORBALS DAYS

I spent many happy years working in the Gorbals in Glasgow. The Irish, Highland and Lowland combination made an eclectic mix. I am not saying it was tough, but the policemen always walked in twos—sometimes hand in hand—and that was in the police station.

The *craic* was excellent, before the days of PC, AC/DC and audits.

A patient who had known my children asked after their well-being:

'Hoo's the weans?' (How are the children?)

'Fine thanks. One's a cop and one's a lawyer.'

'Guid. They're pullin' them in and you're pullin' them oot!'

It made my heart sing.

14 Open wide. This won't hurt a bit!

I bought a pair of new shoes which squeaked annoyingly, so they lay unused in the back surgery. Fitting a denture one day, I noticed a hole in a patient's shoe.

'What size do you take?'

'Eights.'

'Here's a pair going spare.'

For the next month, I was asked by various patients for:

'Brown, size 8' and

'a new set of *wallies*[1].'

§§§§

It was happy hour in the dental department of the Gorbals Health Centre. The idea was to set aside an hour of the working day for toothaches, eases and dressings. Patients did not need a prior appointment, rather than a happy hour where I take out two teeth for the price of one!

This patient was different—not special—just different. His examination was no problem. I concluded he needed one extraction (the tooth was only fit for the bucket), two fillings and a scale and polish to see him dentally fit. My patient was not happy about having an extraction.

'Are you sure you can't save this tooth?' he asked several times.

After thinking about it, my patient asked diffidently if he could have a second opinion. I asked that if he found a dentist who could save that tooth, I would appreciate it if he or she could get back in touch with me to tell me how they could do it. I was very sure no-one could save that one. My patient left to seek his second opinion.

Later, as I left for lunch, I walked through the waiting room and saw my second opinion patient, sitting quietly with head bent, hands clasped in prayer. The receptionist whispered to me, 'He's asking for his second opinion.' Afterwards, I was so glad that the Lord agreed with my diagnosis, as my patient went off happily clutching his offending molar in a paper towel.

One day, ten-year-old twins who had never been to a dentist before attended my surgery. I saw one twin whilst the other waited. 'Jump up into the chair and put your head on the rest, please,' I said, turning around to glance at my patient's new blank card. I turned back to do and say something light and easy to put the youngster at ease to find he had jumped up as

---

[1] dentures

requested, but put his chin in the headrest, facing the back of the chair. Realising we had a problem here, I was more careful to explain to the other twin what was expected.

After that examination I asked this twin to rinse out. Upon this request, my so-very-new-to-dentistry patient ignored the mouthwash and squirmed about over the spittoon until he could reach the tiny water pipe which constantly ran to cleanse the sink. Compassion overcoming hilarity, I demonstrated with the mouthwash tumbler.

After some weeks, the twins left dentally fit and completely *au fait* with the workings of a dental surgery.

§§§§§

On another occasion, I had a visit from the new head honcho, a new broom whose orders were to make cuts in the department. My happy hour was quiet that day; probably a riot or football match—or both—scheduled in Glasgow somewhere. When I stuck my head out of the surgery, the waiting room was full of suits. Normally, anyone wearing a suit and tie in my waiting room would be called The Accused! However, these guys had VIP stamped on their foreheads.

Withdrawing suspiciously fast, I asked, 'Who are they?' of the nurse.

'That's Mr Big and his team from the Health Board,' was hissed at me. You can tell I was well-versed in the local board politics and health centres.

'This waiting room is empty,' the boss man boomed to no-one. (Gee whiz, this guy is really ahead of the game, and Gorbals humour was really called for here).

'Of course it's empty,' I said, coming out to shake hands. 'We cancelled the patients as we thought you would be taking us out for lunch.'

Things progressed rapidly downhill as they toured the department and I was ignored. As the suits left, and feeling I should show some Highland hospitality, I said cheerily, 'Have a nice day, as they say, and let us know when you're coming back and I'll have the coffee pot on.'

An hour later, my immediate boss was on the phone in hysterics. He asked, 'Are you mad? Don't you know Mr Big has no sense of humour?' 'Neither did Hitler, Stalin or Pol Pot, but my parents taught me to treat all God's children the same.'

A year later, one of the medics who organised things at the centre took me aside and said, 'Lachie, do me a favour. Could you not be here next Thursday, as Mr Big is coming?'

'OK,' I said and took the staff down the pub for lunch.

§§§§

One day, all hell broke out at the front desk. Looking out of the surgery, I could see that a middle-aged chap of medium build with a dozen recent stitches in his face was demanding treatment. I moved to the door to pour oil on troubled waters; I was in my serenity phase. The chap in question was tired and depressed, i.e. dangerously under the influence. After much agitation, I manoeuvred him to the door and he let out his last final burst of expletives: 'You're that ******* Hielan' ****'

Grasping him firmly by the lapels, we both fell over onto the floor and were rescued by the nurses and receptionist, whose main concern was for the patient, of course. He vanished into the night with cries of vengeance and murder. News travels fast in the Gorbals. A few days later, another worthy patient approached with, '*Hey Mac, a hear ye use a new method here; instead of makin the dentures fit the mooth, ye mak the mooth fit the dentures.*' I lived on my hard man reputation for many years.

PS: Now retired and wishing I wasn't, I have a lovely house named Dunfillin.

15 Unable to find family in Edinburgh,
I went into a shop and ordered this plaque in a fit of pique!

GÀIDHLIG

Tha 'n còinneach fàsach a' cinntinn nàdar
'S chan fhaic thu làrach nan daoine ciùin;
Le fuadach 's bàirlinn chaidh 'n cur thar sàile,
'S an t-àl a dh'fhàg iad, cha till iad ruinn.

> *The wild moss is growing freely*
> *Erasing traces of the people's homes;*
> *With expulsions and summons they were sent abroad,*
> *And their people will not return to us.*

'An t-Eilean Àlainn'
Seumas Dòmhnallach

NUAIR BHA MI ÒG

Ceud bliadhna air ais!

Rugadh mise anns an Ògmhios agus thòisich an dàrna cogadh anns an fhoghair. Sin a thuirt mo phiuthar, Maighread, anns an leabhar *Lachann Dubh a' Chrògain. AMF (all my fault)* a-rithist—beagan feargach a sin!

Chaidh mi gu sgoil a' Bhaile Ghrunndail anns an eilean, Àrd-sgoil an Òbain, 's a sin gu Oilthigh Chill Rìbhinn. Carson Oilthigh Chill Rìbhinn? Cha robh àite anns na feadhainn eile!

Cha robh mòran dhaoine ann an Achadh na Croise nuair a bha mise beag, ach cha mhòr nach eil fichead taigh a sin a-nis. Baile Mòr gu dearbh. Bha mi a' coiseachd mìle na dhà don sgoil agus an toiseach bha mo charaid Dòmhnall MacIlleDhuibh leam. Bha esan deich bliadhna nas sine na mise agus bha e mòr, cuideachd.

'Tha mo chasan beaga goirt, a Dhòmhnaill,' theireadh mise, agus thogadh esan mi air a dhruim. Nuair a bha mi mu chòig-bliadhn'-deug a dh'aois bhitheadh e ag èisteachd ris an sgeulan thruaighe a bha agam.

'An do chaochail duine?'

'O Dhia, cha do chaochail.'

'Ach ma-tà, bidh e ceart gu leòr ann an seachdain, ma-tha.'

Bha m' athair dà fhichead sa trì deug 's mo mhàthair da fhichead 's a trì nuair a thàinig mise, ach bha an taigh daonnan làn le daoine, ceòl agus leabhraichean. Tha fhios gun robh mi aonarach gun chloinn anns a' bhaile, ach bha mi glè shona leam fhèin.

'Balach beag math,' thuirt mo mhàthair ris na daoine a thigeadh anns an t-samhradh. 'Tha e suidheadh aig an doras 's e cluich leis fhèin!' (*playing by myself, Mother, not with myself*). Bha iad ag àrach le iongantas air am balach beag trì bliadhna a dh'aois!

Sìos a' chladaich ag iasgach le prìne na suas a' bhruaich airson slat 's mi ag obrach air bogha-saighde.

Cha robh mi toigheach (amaideach) air a' phìob mhòr (*Highland war pipes*) ach bha an *accordion* uarraidh math airson dannsadh ris.

Cha robh dealan anns an eilean beag Liosach gu 1970 's bha eagal orm ro na bòcain agus ro Mharsaili Mhòir.

'Suas an staidhre,' theireadh mo mhàthair. 'Tha mi ag iarraidh mo speuclairean.' Bha e dorcha 's bha mise suas agus sìos an staidhre coltach ri coinean.

'Dè tha ceàrr air a' bhalach sin,' thuirt m' athair.

'Ach, bidh e leis na *growing pains*,' thuirt mo mhàthair.

Bha mi glè bheag gus an do ruig mi ceithir-deug.

'Tha e uarraidh caol,' thuirt mo mhàthair ris an nurs, is eagal oirre ro TB.

'Chan eil,' thuirt an nurs, 'ach tha e *wiry*.'

Oh nach robh i math, cha mhòr nach do phòg mi i.

Bha mi coiseachd leis mo bhroilleach a-mach coltach ri coileach.

'Tha mi *wiry*. Tha mi *wiry*.'

Tha mi fàs sean a-nis, ach bha mi riamh sealbhach: ach nach robh a h-uile Dòmhnallach à Earra-Ghàidheal a chaidh a thogail leis a' Ghàidhlig: cainnt Ghàrradh Eden? Cha bhi mòran de na feadhainn eile ann!

Seo crìoch air an t-searmon.

16 Balach beag math?
(Were you in the sheep dip?—Ed)

LACHUNN A' PHEIGI

Fhuair mi an sgeul seo bho m' athair, Seumas Dòmhnallach, nuair a bha mi aig an àrd-sgoil anns an Òban.

Mun bhliadhna 1867, bha duine bho Liosmòr dom b' ainm Lachann Dòmhnallach ann an luing mhòir a bha a' seòladh mu chòrsaichean an iar Astràilia. Aon oidhche nuair a bha am bàta air acair ann an camas aibhne, thàinig long spùinnidh ri a cliathaich, agus ann am beagan ùine bha smachd aig na daoine fhiadhaich sin air Lachann bochd agus sgioba a' bhàta. Thòisich am muirt. Thug na spùinneadairean-mara sgioba na luinge, aon air dèidh aoin, gu deireadh a' bhàta eile am fianais duine mòr a bha na sheasamh an sin agus an dèidh sin bha iad a' tilgeil nan daoine bochd thar a' chliathaich. Thàinig iad airson Lachann: nuair a bha solas na combaist air aodann, thuirt an duine mòr seo ri a sgioba fhèin: 'Thigibh an seo leis an duine sin.' Rinn iad sin agus cha robh Lachann a' faicinn anns an dorchadas ach gun robh feusag mhòr leathann air an duine. 'A Lachainn,' thuirt easan, 'nach bitheadh e math a bhith ann an Liosmòr ag iasgach sgadain am Port nam Mòr-laoch a-nochd. Cha d' fhuair Lachann riamh sealladh air aodann an duine, ach an ath latha chuir iad air tìr e agus ràinig e an taigh aig beul na h-oidhche.

Anns na bliadhnaichean a chaidh seachad, thàinig Lachann dhachaigh gu Liosmòr, phòs e, agus bha aon mhac dom b-ainm Ùisdean aige. Bha am balach seo ro dhuilich aig uairean agus bha e daonnan a' dèanamh rudan cronail, coltach ri a bhith ceangal ri chèile earball nan damh. Aon latha, anns an t-Sàilean, nuair a bha Lachann fo a' bhàta, a' *Pheigi*, le paipear-naidheachd aig uileann agus a' toirt tacan a' leughadh agus tacan a' glanadh a' bhàta, thàinig a mhac agus chuir e teine ris a' phàipeir.

'Trobhad, a laochain,' thuirt athair agus fhuair e greim air ròpa agus nuair a thàinig na fir a bha ag obair anns an ath-aol a bhacadh Lachann bhon ghnìomh uabhasach seo, bha an ròpa thairis air craobh le lùb-ruith air. Dh'fhaodte nach robh e ach a' gabhail air—dh'fhaodte.

17 An Sàilean (tràth san 20mh linn)

Madainn Didòmhnaich bha na fir trus aig doras na h-eaglaise agus ghlaodh fear dhuibh nuair a thàinig laoch dlùth, 'Seo Lachann Dòmhnallach, companach aig Ned Kelly.'

'Thig a seo, a bhalaich, 's thèid sinn air son sràid,' thuirt Lachann ris an fhear cham. Chaidh iad null ar cùl na h-eaglaise agus cha tàinig iad air ais airson an t-searmoin. Thàinig droch chuimhne air an fhear sin, agus cha robh fhios aige air nì idir, idir bhon àm sin!

Aon latha, nuair a bha m' athair dhachaidh bho na bàtaichean *dynamite*, chaidh e staigh air chèilidh air Lachann.

'A bheil fhios agad dè tha ceàrr orm?' thuirt am bodach bhon leabaidh.

'Ach, chan eil ann ach an seann aois,' thuirt Seumas le beagan critheanach na ghuth. 'Tha thu ceart gu leòr,' thuirt am fear eile!

Shiubhail an duine seo na sheann dhuine mun bhliadhna 1910 ann an Sròn na Craoibhe. Tha e air a thiodhlacadh anns a' Chlachan, agus gus an latha an-diugh, chì thu a' chlach le ainm air an sin.

PARA SHANDAIDH

Bha mòran *puffers* a' tighinn gu Liosmòr nuair a bha mise òg, a' cur air tìr gual ann am Port Ramasa agus Achadh na Croise.

O Dhia, 's ann a sin a bha an hòro-gheallaidh: bodaich a' glaodhaich, na coin a' dol gòrach, agus h-uile duine cho dubh ris an diabhal. Na cairtean is na Fergie *tractors* a' dol le gual don a h-uile taigh.

Cha bhiodh boireannaich a-riamh a' dol sìos don cheidhe agus tha fhios agad gun robh na seòladairean gealtach ro mhnathan le falt ruadh, ministearan agus mucan! Bha falt ruadh air mo mhàthair agus rachadh i staigh nuair a bha na fir a' dol a-mach anns a' bhàta.

Aon oidhche, bha plaideachan a' tiormachadh air a' chnoc is ghlaoidh mise, 'tha an t-uisge a' tighinn,' is ruith ise a-mach nuair a bha Seonaidh Bàn a' dol seachad leis na slatan-iasgaich air a ghualainn.

'O tha mi duilich, a Sheonaidh,' thuirt ise.

'Ceart gu leòr, a Pheigi,' thuirt esan, is chaidh e dìreach dhachaidh. Bha an t-iasg sàbhailte an oidhche sin.

Bha mise a' leughadh *Para Shandaidh* òg, is a rithist san oilthigh, agus an-sin dhà no trì bliadhna air ais, 's a h-uile àm tha rudeigin ùr ann. Bha mòran do m' dhaoine aig muir, 's bha m' athair is bràthair m' athair nan sgiobairean air na bàtaichean ICI—*Dynamite Boats* mar a theireadh iad.

A h-uile oidhche, nuair a chaidh iad an laighe, bha m' athair a' leughadh *Para Handy and Other Tales*, no am Bìoball, gu mo mhàthair.

'An cuala tu am fear seo?' Hurricane Jack no An Tar (chuala ise e fichead uair) is bhitheadh easan a' gàireachdainn; chan ann leis a' Bhìoball, tha thu a' tuigsinn.

<fuaim srannail>

'Tha thu nad chadal a-rithist.'

<brag>

Sìos leis an leabhair.

'I'm wasting my time here.'

<sàmhchair >

A-nis 's mi làithean san 'yat' air acair mu na h-eileanan an iar—tha mise a' glaodhaich, 'Cluinn seo, a bhalachaibh,' ris na companaich agam 's tha na sgeulachdan aig Neil Munro beò fhathast.

Thàinig cearcall a' chuain mun cuairt a-rithist?

BEURLA

For those not yet acquainted with the language of the Garden of Eden, here are loose translations of the above. The exception is *Nuair a Bha Mi Òg*, as all the elements can be found threaded throughout the rest of the book. Anyone who correctly marries any of the *Gàidhlig* with its English counterpart will be awarded a special prize: afternoon tea with the author (answers on a postcard, please—Ed).

LACHUNN A' PHEIGI

I got this story from my father, James MacDonald, when I was at Oban High School.

About the year 1868, a man from Lismore was sailing in a ship off the coast of Australia. One evening, when she was anchored for night, she was boarded by savage pirates from a fast cutter, and who captured the crew. The murder began. The crew were taken one by one to the stern where the pirate skipper was standing with their hands tied and then thrown over the side. They came for Lachlan, when the light of the compass fell on his face, the pirate skipper said, 'bring that man here.' In the darkness, Lachlan could only see that he was a big man with a beard.

'Lachlan,' said the man, in Gaelic, 'would it not be great to be in Lismore, fishing herring in Port nam Mòr-laoch tonight?' Lachlan was taken below and never saw the man again, but in the morning he was put ashore and found a house that evening.

It is highly unlikely that anyone but a Lismore man would know of a wee bay called Port nam Mòr-laoch behind Port Ramsay.

In the years that followed, Lachlan came back to Lismore, married, and had one son called Ùisdean. This boy was badly behaved and was constantly getting up to tricks like putting clods over the chimney or tying bullocks' tails together and driving his father and mother demented.

Lachlan came home with money and bought a house and land at the Crossroads and a small pleasure yacht, the *Peggy*. This was most unusual as most were work boats. One day, Lachlan was lying under his boat in Sàilean tarring her bottom and Ùisdean was larking about while Lachlan read *The Oban Times* and having a blast at his pipe; other times he did a spot of work. Suddenly, Ùisdean set fire to the newspapers.

'Come here, my little hero' said his father and, grabbing the boy and a rope, put a running noose on it and threw the end over the limb of a tree.

The men working in the lime quarry came running down, shouting, 'What on earth is going on?'

'Ach I was just teaching the boy a lesson,' said Daddy, calmly.

Perhaps he was—perhaps.

One Sunday, the men had congregated as usual for a smoke outside the church before the service, when they were joined by a chap who had just come back from Australia. He was a loud-mouthed fellow and said, on seeing Lachlan, 'Well, Well, Lachie MacDonald, Ned Kelly's right-hand man.'

Showing no emotion, Lachlan said, 'Come,' and they went for a walk instead of going to church. This chap seemed to lose his memory and claimed it was a case of mistaken identity. Lachlan's reputation rose and people were nervous of his presence. This was not helped when a bunch of lads took their father's brand new lantern and put it over Lachlan's father's grave in the cemetery at night. They knew Lachlan passed on his way home from a friend's house and they hid in the bushes.

'Well, well, I wonder if the old fellow wants to talk to me tonight,' said Lachlan in a loud voice. He walked up to the grave, lifted the lantern and went home with it! The boys had some explaining to do.

Father was home on leave and the word came that Lachlan wanted to see him. With some trepidation, he approached the man in the bed.

'I believe you have some medical knowledge, James, so what's the matter with me?'

'I am a third mate and only have first aid knowledge, but perhaps it's old age?'

'Quite right,' said the man in the bed, and father breathed again.

Lachlan died an old man, at Stronacraoibh around the year 1910. He is buried in Clachan, and to this day you can see his gravestone with his name on it.

PARA HANDY

There are very few puffers left round the Disunited Kingdom these days. As far as I am aware, there is a VIC (victualling inshore craft) in Crinan and another being refurbished there. They built about fifty of these between 1939 and 1945 and after the Second World War they were going cheap and this was really their heyday. 'The Crinan Canal for Me' was a popular song then, and I can heartily agree when it's blowing and I am as sick as a dog.

The puffers started their life in canals and were simple barges pulled by horses. Then they put simple steam engines in them like locomotives so that the steam escaped and made the 'puff-puff' noise. Then came the condensing engines which recycled the steam, thus saving on water and increasing efficiency; by this time, they were metal and had a forecastle for'ard and a wheelhouse aft. By this time, they had grown seaworthy and could go anywhere even where there were no piers because they were flat-bottomed and could take the ground.

Once the ro-ros[1] came, the day of the puffer was finished.

When I was wee, puffers were common at Port Ramsay and Achnacroish. They normally discharged coal, although with their derrick and winch they could handle any cargo. This was obvious in the film *The Maggie*, when the cargo was expensive furniture for the Yankee's house.

The women stayed well away from the pier when the puffer came because:
1. superstition
2. makeup.

I love the story of my red-haired mother meeting *Seonaidh Bàn* on his way to the fishing. Oh, that we had retained these beliefs instead of politicians and managers.

---

[1] roll-on roll-off (ferries)

I read *Para Handy* young because my father did, then at university, and recently for the third time. There are so many layers of humour in there, especially for people who knew the puffer men and that whole scene. There are very few books that make me laugh out loud: *Thoughts of Murdo* by Iain Crichton Smith and some of Bill Bryson's do as well.

At one stage, about a hundred years ago, they said that 50% of the adult male population from the western Scottish islands were at sea. You don't eat well with only a croft to sustain you.

Every night, when Mother and Father went to bed, he would read either *Para Handy* or the Bible. You could hear him laughing at the exploits of Hurricane Jack or The Tar—not at the Bible.

'Have you heard this one, mother?' (She had, about twenty times before.)

Sound of snoring.

'Woman! You have fallen asleep again.'

Bang would go the book on the bedside table and he would blow out the lamp. Father died a week or two after electricity came to Lismore.

Nowadays, when we are lying at anchor somewhere bombproof in the Western islands, I sometimes shout to the companions in the yacht, 'listen to this one,' and read out Para Handy's exploits. The tales of Neil Munro live on. The circle of the sea has come around again.

ESSAYS, ARTICLES AND STORIES
Not necessarily in any particular order

COMANN EACHDRAIDH LIOS MÒR

An island of fewer than 200 souls, Lismore has grown vulnerable and fragile over the years. As in the rest of the country, any industries have gone, fishing and farming are in decline, and there is little chance of Lismore becoming the silicon glen of the West. For continuing existence as a viable island, we are talking tourism, and anything which is positive in encouraging this is a huge asset to the community as a whole.

The survival of Gaelic in a small Inner Hebridean island like Lismore is partly due to a core of native Gaelic-speaking *Liosaich* (people of Lismore) whose knowledge, understanding and feeling for their culture bears no relation to formal education or status within the workforce or society. This, compounded with the wealth of literature and song by ministers, deans, bards, master mariners, farmers, academic researchers (once expressed by Diane of the latter, 'they are about as numerous in the Highlands as midges,

18 Ionad Naomh Moluag, Comann Eachdraidh Lios Mòr

and as useful') and even the occasional exciseman, make available prolific material quite unique within—and to—Scotland.

Comann Eachdraidh Lios Mòr has poured resources, manpower and an enormous amount of hard work into the venture over the past few years. The potential of *Lios Mòr* (meaning, in Gaelic, the big garden) combined with the *Comann Eachdraidh* is economically viable. The interest of our cousins overseas has never been greater and these people are hungry for roots in an unstable and insecure world. People want to know more than ever who they are and where they come from, and are willing to pay for this information; man cannot live by bread alone!

The *Comann Eachdraidh* is a living, working force for the growth and continuation of our cultural heritage. We now have people from all over the UK—and beyond—working and living in Lismore. The new crofters have integrated with the island and added to the richness of our small community. At the beginning, all matters and all discussions were in Gaelic and we were proud of this; nowhere else but Lewis in the Outer Isles could say this! It was felt, however, that unless we used English too, then we were limiting ourselves and excluding a large part of the population, many of whom had expertise, skills, time, and energy to contribute.

Comann Eachdraidh Lios Mòr involves all ages to give the island a new solidarity that it so badly needed for a prosperous future. The future is bright—the future is ethnic!

AN SGIOBAIR
THE CAPTAIN

My father James was born in Oban, Argyllshire in 1885, and the crofters received tenure in 1886, but as far as I can tell, there is no connection between these two facts. His siblings Jessie, John and Lachie were born on Lismore, but he did not speak a lot about his own father, John, who was deep sea for most of his life, along with half of the island males, and had voyages on the *Ariel* and the *Cutty Sark*. There is some scuttlebutt in the family that Grandfather liked to quench his thirst after a long voyage, but—what the hell—salt water makes a man thirsty!

Grandfather was known as the Lord and whether this was a reference to *his* grandfather who had money, land and a two-master, or to the fact that they were now reduced to two acres and a cow (wee bit of Highland humour), no-one knows.

19 Captain James MacDonald, my father

When Grannie was an old lady, sunning herself at the end of the house, a 'holy roller' tried to get her to join his band. Getting fed up, she shuffled into the house to the cries of the preacher, 'Do you know the Lord?' Over her shoulder, she retorted, 'I certainly should; I've been married to him for 40 years!'

John MacDonald died in Lismore in 1930, and his wife, Sarah Livingstone, in 1938. Father spoke a lot about his maternal grandfather, *Lachunn Dubh a' Chrògain* (dark-haired Lachlan from Croggan in Mull), Lachlan Livingstone, who was known as the Mull bard. My father spent many holidays with him in Croggan. It was from him that father and his brothers inherited their love and skills in music and *bàrdachd*[1].

Father grew up in Port Ramsay, a hamlet of a dozen houses which produced half a dozen master mariners in as many years. His school years were fragmented and he left school at 14, barely able to read and write. There were 70 pupils in the school at Baligarve, and the older scholars worked as helpers teaching the young ones, so education was a bit hit or miss in those days. Over his adult years, he addressed this and ended his career as a master mariner with the ICI Nobel shipping line (known to us as Nobel's).

20 Port Ramsay today

Father started off his working life with a job sailing and rowing a 15-foot skiff on the Appin ferry. This could not have been easy, as his family referred to him as *am fear caol* (the thin fellow). Although he put on muscle as he grew, he was only 5 feet 6 inches fully stretched. In his words, his next job was on a 'dirty, rotten, old smack.'

[1] poetry

Dunfillin

21 James MacDonald as a young man (assistant ferryman) aged between 14 and 16. This rowing boat—skiff—is 12 to 13 feet in length and took passengers over from Lismore to Port Appin. The rig is called a dipping lug sail.

22 James MacDonald on the right of the photograph with Mr MacAskill the ferryman in the bow of the boat.

One night, leaving Port Ramsay laden with lime, a south-westerly gale sprang up. His father at daybreak walked across Lismore to Kilcheran to see if she was still afloat. Having been at sea all his life, he knew where the boat might be if she had not gone down in the gale. They were safe, having dropped anchor in the shelter of the Kilcheran islands.

Father's next couple of years' employment was on a steam yacht called the *Ilona*. These craft were in abundance before the First World War. He sometimes boasted, with a cloth over his shoulder, about his time as a steward, although with his background, he would have been much better on deck. With a twinkle in his eye, when my mother was in Oban for the day and Father was in charge of the cooking, he used to call himself chief cook and bottlewasher.

A couple of deep sea trips later and in his next employment he had an occasion with a cargo of oranges; he assured us there was no scurvy on that trip! But what there was, unfortunately, was a bully mate[2] aboard who gave my father a very hard time of it. Most of the crew were *Leòdhasaich* (Lewismen). They were older and much larger than my father, but it was not the done thing to interfere. However, getting tired of this, one of the crew, a semi-pro boxer, picked a fight with the mate, who was throwing his weight around as usual and gave him a good thrashing which he richly deserved. There was no more trouble.

§§§§§

Working with a couple of big-made Irish brothers came next. They owned a puffer/coaster called the *Peerie*. Father thought they were totally off the wall, but very kind. They called him Friday because he just appeared one morning, he was small, a bit sallow-skinned and spoke Scottish Gaelic fluently—a bit like Robinson Crusoe's Man Friday as described by Daniel Defoe.

One Christmas, they took father home with them to Glasgow. With a few drams on the way, presents and a Christmas tree which they dragged onto a tram and then up a close, they burst into a house full of women and children. The brothers walked around the table a couple of times, and then out, leaving Father on his own, not introduced to anyone. My father, being a very sociable person, fitted in just fine with the *craic* and singing a couple of Gaelic songs to his new audience.

[2] enforcer

One Sunday, in a wee pram dinghy, the elder of the two brothers was rowing the younger ashore to attend church. Nearing the shore, the elder brother asked if he had a chow of tobacco, and as soon as the younger shoved his hands in his pocket to find it, his brother cowped the dinghy. The younger, religious brother, soaking wet, waded ashore, shook himself like a dog and continued his way to church. His brother picked him up after the service and not a word was exchanged.

There was an ending to this story. Twenty years later, father was ashore and he saw the old *Peerie* lying alongside the quay. It looked dilapidated and deserted, apart from a wisp of smoke from the forecastle chimney. Just for a bit of sport, he had handy a firework picked up from where he worked now at Nobel's. He jumped quietly aboard and deftly slipped his powerful Thunderflash (made especially powerful for the army by Nobel's), down the chimney. A loud bang and a puff of smoke followed by silence made him wonder about the old fellow who used to sit by the stove every night reading the *Sporting News* and smoking his pipe. The silence went on for too long. He wondered if the fright had killed one or both of them; they were old men now. 'Oh God! Have I killed the old men? They were so good to me when I was a boy and learning my trade!'

Eventually, the hatch opened and a soot-encrusted face appeared, shouting, 'Friday! I know that is you! Come down here and I promise not to kill you!' Father, hiding behind the coal waggons on the pier, shouted back, 'Yes you will! I'll come back and see you in the morning!'

Father being a ship's mate at the time had access to ship's gear. Friday went round the next day with ropes, paint and provisions. The old fella had cooled down by now and Father was welcomed aboard. One feels that some strong stimulant had been taken that night, but you had to make your own entertainment in those days, and the Irish always loved a joke.

§§§§

Tickets—they were certificates for passing maritime exams—were taken at the Nautical College in Glasgow, and lodgings had to be found. On one occasion, Father said the landlady fed him minced horse at every meal. His face grew longer and hair started growing down the back of his neck; he went off mince.

§§§§§

Working for Nobel, James spent time on the SS *Lady Dorothy*, the *Lady Anstruther* and he became skipper of the SS *Lady Gertrude Cochrane*. His brother Lachlan followed as skipper a few years later.

§§§§§

Father married twice. His first wife Bella was from Coll. They had no children, and Bella died from TB, which was rife on the West Coast at the time. In 1928 he married my mother, Margaret (Peggy) Buchanan from Lismore. She had three brothers: Hugh, Donald and John. Donald was killed in the First World War at Ypres and is remembered on the Menin Gate Memorial. John and Hugh survived the war.

When my father died, and my mother and I were arranging his funeral, she asked me where I thought father would like to be buried. My response was Lismore, since he had retired here and it was here he had lived his last years. My mother asked if I thought he would like to be buried in Irvine beside his first wife. Sad to say, I snapped back, 'Don't be ridiculous. You gave him his children and many good years.' But later, when thinking this over, I had to give my mother the benefit of being a gracious and feeling individual.

§§§§§

James was the last of the great storytellers on the island. He had a gift which is sadly dying out as radio, television and all the other media take over. He loved working with Nobel's which became ICI in the 1930s and he had many sea tales to tell. One story related to crossing the North Sea one fine night and fits in with the walls of water reported by numerous fishermen over the years. He was at the wheel with his chum Bobby who was Third Mate. They heard a hissing sound and a wall of water appeared which broke halfway up the mast. The weight of water rolled her on her side, but they had not reduced speed; there was no time.

The firemen were praying as the water spewed down the ventilators; they thought they were on the bottom. Slowly the water cleared and she came back up. If there had been another wave, she would have turned turtle. As she regained speed, the captain's door opened; it was positioned below the open bridge and they could smell the aromatic tobacco he smoked in his pipe.

Then the door closed, not a word spoken. He did not come up on the bridge; his trust in my father and his other officers was implicit.

§§§§§

One winter he was caught amongst the ice floes off Hamburg with a deck cargo of nitro-glycerine, which is very unstable and can be set off by even a slight bump. It was a huge responsibility; if the ship blew up, so would a large part of Hamburg.

This and other similar factors led my father to have what was known in those days as a nervous breakdown in the 1930s and again later in the 1950s. But, as the coast guard and the leader of the home guard for Lismore in World War II, he seemed A1 to me.

§§§§§

Father was still very active when I was growing up and he shot everything that moved and caught anything that swam. I was not allowed out fishing in the evenings until I was ten or eleven. Fishing from the small boat was in the summer, April to October, and winter fishing was off the rocks (after baiting the ground) or in the fresh water lochs on the island.

Just before Christmas, if the weather let us, we found holly bushes on *an t-Eilean Dubh* (the Black Isle) for the decorations. Father gave my mother posies of the Grass of Parnassus, a small white flower which grows in wet areas of Lismore. We believed it only grew in Lismore and Israel, but I have been told it can grow in other parts of the north of the UK, Ireland and other places.

Father was still singing at mods and ceilidhs until he was in his mid-sixties. He represented Lismore as a councillor for many years when the council met in Ballachulish. He had a late burst of songwriting about this time. The Captain was particularly good at songs which were humorous, and he wrote music for some of them. About 1952, he said to me one day, '*Lachuinn*, both my brothers have written songs for Lismore. It's about time I wrote one too.' In contrast to the songs of his brothers, which praised Lismore's beauty in great detail, Father's song, 'An t-Eilean Àlainn' (The Lovely Island), describes the real state of affairs on the island.

Also, I have recently discovered some 2/4 marches which are good, according to David, a piping maestro living in Lismore. My father had stopped piping during the Second World War and taken up the piano. He offered my mother a fur coat as a gift, which she refused as she considered them to be 'common', and wanted a piano instead. At times like New Year, when he was into reels and jigs, he would stand up and attack the piano with great enthusiasm, the ornaments on top would start dancing too and Mother would rush forward to rescue them. The piano top was also lined with glasses of whisky from the first-foots, from which Father had taken a sip, for politeness' sake. When the first-footers had left, he would pour the whisky into a bottle to keep it as medicine for colds, coughs, chills, flu, broken legs and so on for the coming year.

James liked doing things well: 100% every time. He was also not a good audience, watching others doing things he used to do himself. Sometime during my teenage years, he stopped fishing, shooting and singing (at concerts). He kept active and read a lot, especially sea tales. He had a louder voice than most, being used to giving orders from an open bridge in bad weather.

Father seemed to have the knack of picking the worst days to go to Oban. The ferry, named MV *Lochnell*, had been an ambulance boat on the Clyde during the Second World War, and would set off in a cloud of spray, much to the understandable dismay of my mother (her own father had been drowned at sea). The *Lochnell* had lighter engines put in after the war and

23 MV *Lochnell* at Lismore Pier

was slightly down by the head so that her small wheelhouse forward would disappear in water when there was a sea running. The *Lochnell* lay in Ballachulish at the end of her career until she sank in the 1980s.

Sometimes in Oban, Father would meet an ex-opera singer who had no work for a while and had been taken over by *uisge beatha*[3]. The two men would retire up a close and swap songs. The Captain did not drink, but was not a shy person, and would burst into song in an instant whilst my mother hastened to the other end of the town!

§§§§

One day in Gigha, years after my father had died, I was sitting beside a lady in a café who, on finding out about me and where I came from, told me this tale.

Some time ago, she had been a telephonist in the Oban exchange. In those days when you phoned you would be put through to the number you wished. She knew my father's voice so well she used to say to him, 'I'll put you through, Captain, if you sing me a Gaelic song first.' So he did, at full volume, in a public telephone box. These days, with Big Brother watching you, it would be the jail, or at least a caution for disturbance of the peace.

§§§§

I made him the best pair of new dentures ever, although my father was a terrible patient even just for *wallies*. (I extracted most of my mother's lower teeth and gave her an immediate denture at the age of 82 with much less fuss.) Eventually, we won the day. My mother told me some time later that he kept them wrapped in a linen hankie in his top pocket and wore his old ones. When he met anyone he knew, even vaguely, he would pull out the dentures from his pocket, show them off and say proudly that his son, the dental surgeon, made them for him.

When I was working in a small town in Northants, my mother was ill and when my sister took her to her home to nurse her, the Captain flew down on his own, aged 80 and stayed for a holiday with us. Apparently, he had very nice chats with the female cabin crew! It was a bit hair-raising, as he had no worries about the traffic and would march across the road and hold up his

[3] whisky

hand to stop any cars coming towards him. He did not dither about but even so, nowadays, they would have just driven over the top of him.

When Father was suffering from pneumonia, a skipper—for whom my father did not care too much—came to visit him at hospital in Oban. The visitor asked, *'Dè an aois a tha thu a-nis, a Sheumais?'* (What age are you now, James?)

'Ceithir fichead 's a ceithir' (Eighty-four), said Father.

'Och well, you've had a good run for your money,' said the chap.

The patient sat up in bed with his blue eyes blazing. 'You are a stupid man, you always were a stupid man and I don't know how you ever passed your Master's ticket in the first place.'

The poor man left swiftly, with my mother muttering that he was 'only making conversation', but my father was not to be pacified easily. 'He's an ignorant man, as were all his people.' I thought of Dylan Thomas's lines: 'do not go gentle into that good night.'

My wife was most impressed on her last visit to see my father before he died. She had brought the children in to see him too, although our wee boy was too young to know what was happening; our daughter, who always was perspicacious, although very young, was instantly upset to see her *seanair*[4] so ill. She held his hand, and he looked at her, then up at our wee boy in my wife's arms, and said to my wife, 'You have given me so much more than I ever expected. Thank you.' He meant our children, of course; the line will go on.

I once asked my father why he had not become an elder of the church, since he had been the precentor[5] and he had been asked several times to become an elder. His answer was that he was not good enough. 'I think you are setting the bar too high, Father.' He just smiled and shook his head.

Captain James MacDonald, after a full, interesting and good life, died a few days later, in Oban, where he was born, at age 84. I hope he had a peaceful passage and calm blue seas to sail on in *Tìr nan Òg*[6].

---

[4] grandfather

[5] in the Gaelic-speaking church, when there is often not a piano or organ, someone who sings the lines first and the congregation follows, singing the same line

[6] the land of the ever-young

THE DYNAMITE BOATS

My interest in ICI Nobel[1] and the town of Irvine in Ayrshire stems from the fact that my father and his younger brother Lachie were master mariners with the company and—not least—my sister Margaret was born in the town. Lachie worked with the company until retirement, but my father came ashore because of ill health in the late 1930s.

The Swede Alfred Nobel had companies in Sweden, Finland, Germany and Norway by 1860. The explosive nitro-glycerine (nitro) was advertised in 1865, and trials in 1867 led to a patent the same year. Unable to establish a company in England because of the Explosives Act 1869, Nobel, with John Downie of Fairfield Ships, set up the British Dynamite Company in 1871 on the Ardeer Peninsula in Ayrshire and sent for his chief chemist Alarik Liebeck.

Nitro had first been produced in 1846 by mixing nitric acid, sulphuric acid and glycerol, but this was very unstable. Kieselguhr, found in Skye and Aberdeenshire, is a clay-like material which, when mixed with nitro, produces dynamite which is stable unless used with a detonator. In 1873, nitro was introduced to Scotland, although Nobel had been making it in Sweden for 20 years. The company name was changed to Nobel's Explosives in 1877 and at first rowing boats were used to load the ships lying off Ardeer.

The inhabitants of Irvine were naturally nervous of boats being loaded in the town harbour and, in 1905, the Garnock Wharf was built for safety reasons. At the turn of the century, 1,200 people worked in the factory and this increased to 13,000 by 1917. After World War II, acids, ammonia nitrate

---

[1] The Nobel Prize for physics, chemistry, medicine and peace started in 1901. In 1973 recipient Henry Kissinger (Vietnam War) referred to the military as dumb stupid animals. Tony Blair (Iraq) was nominated for the Nobel Peace Prize in 2004 and in 2009 Barack Obama after being in office for one year got it for International Diplomacy.

24 SS Lady Gertrude Cochrane
(painting by Bobby Bond, my father's shipmate)

and paints were being made. ICI produced a non-nicotine cigarette in the 1960s, but this was soon sidelined by the tobacco companies.

The ICI ship *Lady Anstruther* could make Hamburg to Irvine in 84 hours, Gothenburg to Irvine in 72 hours, and Irvine to London in 62 hours. The *Lady Dorothy* and the *Lady Gertrude Cochrane* were much slower. Uncle Lachie used to say that, towards the end of her sailing life, my father's old ship *Lady Gertrude* was so slow that she was holding up traffic in the English Channel!

25 SS Lady Anstruther
(Photograph: A Weir Collection)

26 SS *Lady Dorothy*
(Photograph: *Ships Monthly*)

In the spring of 1939, all the ICI skippers were sent to Hamburg and were addressed by a high-ranking German naval officer covered in gold braid. 'Gentlemen, it appears that shortly our countries will be at war. All our U-boat commanders have silhouettes of the ICI ships, and if you are torpedoed during the hostilities this will be a mistake. We will resume negotiations when peace is restored. Good afternoon.'

There are existing excellent Luftwaffe aerial photos of Ardeer Explosives Works taken during World War II. No attempt was ever made to attack them, apart from a bomber, off course, which dropped bombs in the area.

In 1941, whilst the *Lady Dorothy* was steaming down the Minch at daybreak, the lookout reported a German U-boat periscope. It tracked them for about fifteen minutes and then submerged. Were they out of torpedoes? Why did he not surface and use his deck-guns? Or was an officer below going through the silhouettes of ICI boats? As first mate, Uncle Lachie said it was the longest fifteen minutes of his life; running was not an option, as the U-boat was faster submerged than the *Lady Dorothy* was on the surface!

During World War II the *Lady Anstruther* was armed with a stern-gun which Lachie said came from the Boer War[2]. When he was skipper, he had

---

[2] Second Boer War, South Africa (1899-1902)

the Royal Navy ratings in his cabin and told them that if they did anything to this gun apart from polishing it, he would have them put ashore. The reason was: one flashback from this old gun and it was goodnight Vienna!

On 21 April 1985 the *Lady Helen*, the last of the company ships and owned now by the National Coal Board, was towed out of Irvine full of redundant explosives and safely scuttled in the Atlantic.

The year before, the tug MV *Garnock,* towing other out-of-date explosives, blew up in the Clyde and is now at the Scottish Maritime Museum in Irvine. The skipper, Monty Macfadyen, a second cousin of mine and a native of Lismore, thankfully escaped serious injury.

James and Lachie had great pride in ICI Nobel. My father was very much a Red Ensign[3] man; Uncle Lachie, like myself, was more of a nationalist. They both used to say that when ICI went down the tubes the rest of the country would follow. Of course, this pride in your company was common back then but, as far as I know, with generous pension provision, the company was very good to its workforce, something sadly lacking nowadays.

[3] flag of the Merchant Navy

MO MHÀTHAIR
MY MOTHER

Highland mothers were quietly in charge and, like Jewish mothers, were overprotective of their male offspring. Mother was so careful that when she took me to the Children's Achnacroish Recreation Centre, she tied me to a swing, and then she ran back and forwards to simulate the action.

Most of my women argue: my wife, my sister, my daughter and my granddaughters. My mother did not have to argue; she said her piece, simply and succinctly with her nose in the air and an aristocratic sniff. I was reading her chapter five from the Big Book of AA one day and said,

'What do you think of that, Mother?'

'They were obviously intelligent people, but there is another big book that your father and I gave you for your 18th birthday.'

'Yes, Mother.'

'Do you still have it?'

'Yes, Mother,' I replied.

Sniffing she said, 'It will be in mint condition!'

It was.

Mother, although giving the impression of being a bit stuck-up and forever telling me when I went out to, *'Cuimhnich air na daoine on tàinig thu!'* (Remember those from whom you have come!) had a strange off-the-wall type of humour.

We had always a dozen or so hens behind the house, so we ate a lot of eggs and chickens. Father, who was an expert at killing things, was in hospital, so the job fell to my mother and me. I eventually caught one, and Mother tried to wring its neck, but only succeeded in stretching it so that it ran about clucking with its head on its shoulder. We caught it again and this time managed to get it to the chopping block, and while I held its head, Mother—after a few warm-up blows—severed it. I fell back, clutching its

27 Fragment of Baligrundle School photograph, 1910-11
Margaret (Peigi) Buchanan, is standing back row, fourth from left. There
was only one teacher, so when you got to her age you taught the wee ones.

head in my hands, my mother fell back with the body and the legs still kicking, and I can see her to this day, with the tears running down her face. Hysteria, sadness or mirth? I suspect a mixture of all three.

My mother threw things like a true female: she never hit the target (watch it—Ed), but on one occasion, picked up a stone and threw it in the general direction of a hen in the garden. The stone hit it above the eye and the bird dropped dead; after that Mother was known as the Chicken Killer!

§§§§§

I think the girls were fit in these days and they loved dancing, but this was before the Hall in Lismore was built, so they used barns and sometimes congregated at the crossroads and danced al fresco to a fiddle. One night, Mother and her chums, Alice and Rachel, walked from Achnacroish to Point Ferry, then over the old Jubilee bridge to the Home Farm for a dance, then back again in the morning. Wow!

Dunfillin

28 John Buchanan, Mother, Donald Buchanan (killed in 1917)

§§§§§

When her brother Hugh Buchanan was widowed, she was surrogate mother to his son Iain for five years until he remarried. He stayed in Kilmacolm and Mother loved it there, as she really liked concrete under her feet and the joys of urban living.

Her brother Donald Buchanan was in the 2nd Battalion Argylls[1]. This unit was in the line of Ypres Salient on the evening of 26 September 1917 during the Third Battle of Ypres[2]. A and C Companies came under heavy shellfire and communications were cut. Donald, a great athlete, volunteered. The OC sent several runners to HQ but only one got through. His friend Charles Cameron, also from Lismore, said he was shot.

---

[1] Argyll and Sutherland Highlanders, also known as the Argyll and Suffering Highlanders
[2] also known as the Battle of Passchendaele

29 Donald Buchanan

We still have his keepsakes, which includes his field bible with the inside covers stained with his blood. Mother was devastated, as they were very close. He wrote a poem before he left Lismore and the last lines seem especially touching and prophetic:

> Fare thee well my home of yore
> I may not see thee any more
> And though I lie on foreign shore
> I love thee still …

I visited the battlefields with friends Robert and Peter some years ago, but got most of the information from Ailsa Clarke (Templeton) who used to live on Lismore and had been a World War I battlefield guide. Ailsa took some earth from the croft house where Donald was born, and tries to return to Ypres and the Somme each year to pay respects to him and another Lismore lad, Sandy, who are remembered there.

My mother set off with some friends to Tyne Cot in 1920; sadly, the charabanc broke down and she never made it. We thank you, Ailsa, and although you never met my mother, I know she thanks you too.

§§§§§

Douglas Keith proposed to mother in 1919, when he came back to Lismore on his way home to Australia. The men were given leave during World War I and front-line soldiers could get to Lismore in two days with fast boats and fast trains. The Commonwealth boys who had relatives in the United Kingdom did that a lot, and Douglas had been to Lismore a few times and had fallen in love.

A few families had been cleared from Achanard on Lismore and these included Keiths, Blacks and Buchanans who went to Australia on the *Red Jacket* sailing ship. Mother was devastated after the death of her brother Donald, and said she would give him an answer within the year.

He was only home a few months when a horse-drawn lumber wagon ran away. He had his wee sister with him. In attempting to jump onto the horses to stop them, he fell and was killed under the wheels. The wee girl was saved and I met her as an old lady the first time I went to Australia. But for a runaway horse, I might have been an Aussie.

§§§§§

My mother's father Hugh Buchanan and his crew, Mr MacCallum, were drowned on 26 April 1923. They were fishing salmon—legally—down at the Kilcheran islands and were taking their catch to Oban when the accident happened. Hugh Buchanan's body was found off Kerrera at Slaterich. This event bonded the two families and Neillie MacCallum his son, who had Down's syndrome. He loved my father, who sang *port-a-beul*[3] and played the squeeze box for him.

§§§§§

My mother and father were married in 1928 and at that time father was captain of the SS *Lady Gertrude Cochrane* based at Ardeer, in Ayrshire. My sister Margaret was born in 1930. I was a surprise and born on 15 June 1939, when father was 53 and mother 43. Maybe it was all the fish they ate.

---

[3] mouth music

30 Margaret and AMF

Margaret says that her lovely little brother was born in June 1939 and World War II started in September! I'm having AMF (all my fault) on my headstone.

§§§§§

Opening my own dental practice in Glasgow, I was strapped for cash and mother said one day I looked *muladach*[4] and asked what was wrong.

'Nothing,' I said.

'Yes, there is,' she said.

And when I told her, she gave me *everything* in her bank account and said, 'pay me back when you can.' Fortunately, I paid her back within the year.

§§§§§

I always stick up for mothers, as most of them do a great job, often against heavy odds. The first time my mother saw me with drink, she said, *'Lachuinn, Chan eil an t-uisge-beatha a' còrdadh riut.'* (Lachlan, the whisky does not agree

---

[4] sad, melancholy

with you), and 25 years later she said, '*A bheil thu fhathast a' dol do na coinneamhan?*' (Are you still going to your AA meetings and seeing your friends there?')

Into two small Gaelic sentences, she had identified the problem and the recovery. This was a woman who had left school at 14 and had no personal experience of drink in the family. I raise a (non-alcoholic) glass to mothers everywhere.

Mother died aged 88 in 1985 and in the last week or two she abandoned her second language—English—and mentally returned to the safety and love of her native language—Gaelic.

31 Margaret (Peigi) Buchanan, my mother

HIGHLAND WOMEN

Father used to say, 'One never speaks about the ladies', which makes this story difficult. I grew up being very attracted to women, and being totally bemused by them. Admittedly, their large egos, and their shunning of the words 'yes' or 'no' (you can't be proved wrong if you don't use them) did not help!

My first love went to Australia and I was heartbroken. A year or so later, a more mature lady took me under her wing. She laughed a lot, but whether it was my gags or my performance, I'll never know, and now at my age, it doesn't really matter.

Traditional Gaelic poets describe women in the classical fashion: raven hair, eyebrows liked arched bows, red ruby lips, neck like a swan, alabaster shoulders, crimson-tipped breasts, as the king of Siam used to say. A fantasy world which fortunately moved into the realities of life.

Big women were handy for carrying peats and sailors into the fishing boats. This kept their feet dry, especially if it was low water. Before the days of piers and slips, launching a boat and then going for days soaking wet to the *tòn* was asking for trouble. My paternal great-grandmother did this, but my mother did not like to talk about it.

The Vikings made a big impression on Highland women. When girls were getting married, the old ladies at home used to say, *'Fear mòr bàn'* (a big fair one) or *'Cha robh ach fear beag dubh'* (just a wee dark-haired man). The Celts versus the Picts? You can see whom they preferred: big, fair men.

My only attempt at a love poem was at university, after being stood up one evening. Sharpening my quill, I began, 'By the fireside, slowly dying …'

'You or the fire?' quoth Jock, my flatmate, interrupting the poetic muse.

'Och tae hell, let's go for a pint!'

The muse had departed and so did we.

Mind you, there are a few cheery songs in Gaelic, especially from the Utter Hebrides but then, after seeing those stark islands, you can see why people needed cheering up. This is very strange, as most love songs consist of blue-eyed sailor boys chasing dark-haired maidens in the shielings. Is it the pentatonic scale or the darkness of the soul? My father precented in *Earra-Ghàidheal*[1] fashion: musical and uplifting.

When I was 20, I thought I understood women. Now in my ninth decade, I realise how foolish I was to think that! There is a certain sameness in the body, but the minds are light years apart. Perhaps the old gags are the best: 'Your hair is lovely and your bum does not look big in that frock.' Maybe the best idea is to agree with the last woman you speak to, but sometimes you never can win!

---

[1] Argyll

VOYAGE TO SLEAT

Piper Angus Nicolson's first CD is entitled *Lassies That Baffle Us*. Thirty-three years ago, his uncle Lachie MacDonald (yes, there are a lot of us about!) and I sailed up to Skye to celebrate his birth with his parents, Peggy and Donnie.

On the return, it turned *gruamach*[1] and I became nervous. Lachie, who is very perceptive and has a droll sense of humour, said, 'I did Higher Maths in Oban High School and I have just figured out that the chances of two Lachie MacDonalds drowning today in a 22-foot yacht are ten thousand to one.' Thank you, Lachie, that's taken a load off my mind.

Angus is to play jigs and reels at my funeral. I know what I said earlier about the Highland war pipes, but this guy is class.

---

[1] sullen, gloomy; dangerous, when applied to the sea

BRINE IN THE BLOOD

I come from a long line of seamen. My Lismore great-grandfather had a full-decked fishing smack that made at least one trip I know of to the Continent. My Mull great-grandfather was the last enumerated bard and piper of Maclean of Lochbuie, as well as being a fisherman. My father and my uncle Lachie were master mariners employed by ICI, sailing out of Irvine, and cousin Dougie MacCorquodale was the commodore of the Northern Lighthouse Ships.

32 All the nice girls love a sailor!
Left to right: Hesperus third mate, Mother, Margie MacAndrew,
Cousin Dougie, AMF, Father

Unfortunately, my maternal grandfather was drowned fishing off Lismore, and my grandmother's two brothers were drowned off Mull. This family background made my mother very nervous of salt water (she preferred pavements, restaurants and theatres). I think she was secretly glad when I failed my Merchant Navy eyesight test, being colour blind on red and green. So instead, I went to work at the enamel face!

When a friend recommended me for the Royal Highland Yacht Club, and being in a frivolous mood when filling in the application form, as answer to the question: 'What are your Highland connections?' my response was: 'My mother's people came to Lismore with St Moluag, but my father's people were incomers to the island from Glencoe.' And when asked: 'What connection do you have with the sea?' I replied: 'All my people were at sea in some connection or another, but at night in the winter with the wind howling in the eaves, I'm glad I'm not.' Whoever read and accepted my application obviously had a sense of humour.

§§§§§

Brought up with a dipping lug sail, outboard, oars and not much money about at the end of the war, it was a 4HP Seagull engine against the wind to the fishing grounds and sail or oars back to Achnacroish. For me, real sailing began in the River Forth in the 1970s, crewing for 15s, Loch Longs and Dragons.

One Sunday, I was foolishly persuaded to go in for the Frostbite Series race off Anstruther in a centreboard dinghy, and with no wetsuit. As we set off, my chum, who had been crewing for a couple of weeks in a racing dinghy, handed me the tiller.

'I normally crew,' I said, 'and in keel boats.'

'Same here.' he said.

After going over in the water three times, we were hauled ashore and a patient of mine who had been witnessing this inglorious performance said to me the following day, 'I thought you would be in hospital.'

It was all racing, as cruising off the Fife coast is not recommended unless you are into coal bins and high-rise flats. The shouting and hysteria present in racing upsets my calm, reflective and balanced nature! However, I did notice that the winning skippers gave directions calmly, with time to spare, and didn't change their minds every two seconds.

§§§§§

I was given a mooring under Dunstaffnage Castle in 1977 from John MacLeod, skipper of the Lismore boat via the chief of the 'big hoose in the trees' and was kept alive on many a Sunday morning with coffee and honey from the Davidsons, whose yacht lay next to mine. You laid down your own moorings in these days; two tyres filled with concrete did the trick until a shackle parted in a gale and *Fraoch Eilean* careered around the bay. A local worthy captured her, borrowed a tractor and dragged her halfway to the castle! It took me two days' hard digging to get two channels deep enough to float her off on the big spring tides.

When the marina arrived at Dunstaffnage, I started bemoaning modernisation, advancement, and softness in general, and bewailing the demise of wooden boats and iron men in particular. My Uncle Lachie, who used to lash his clothes to his head and swim ashore to Skye when he was courting Auntie Jean was a family tale.

My son muttered something about pontoons and showers being good for one at a certain age and, after some reflection, I think he may have a point. We have all the facilities now; VHF, GPS, central heating and loos at a huge expense. Would I swap it all for youth and a Hurley 22? You bet!

DIANE

At a dental reunion after I had been speaking, Diane, who is from Forfar, said, 'I am sick and tired of Lachlan boasting of his Celtic heritage and I would like to point out that it was my people, the Picts, who prevented the Romans from subjugating the Scots as they did the English.'

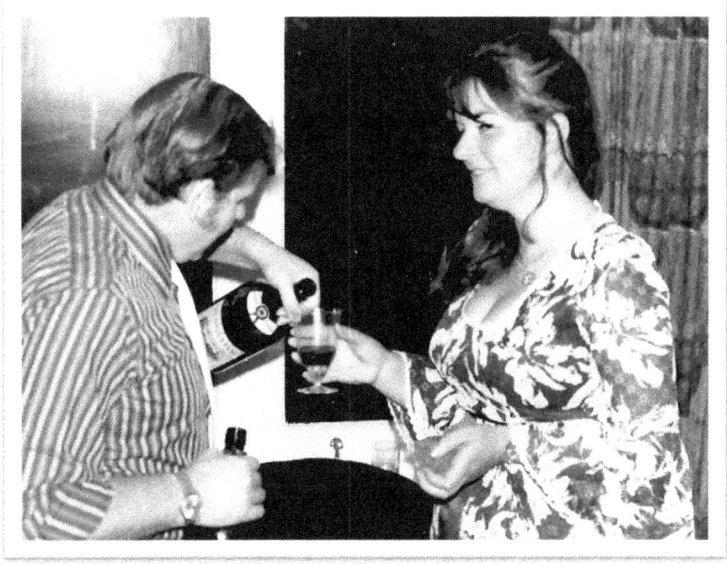

33 This is a lovely photo of Diane, with Jimmie Macdonald, my boss in Kirkcaldy for many years

SEÒNAID

It's a lot easier sailing with Seònaid than a lot of folk I know. She shows no fear and does not give me instructions all the time!

I bought a new Yamaha 9.9 for the Hurley 22 *Salvo* in whom I probably felt more comfortable than a lot of boats. I made and fitted a spray hood which gave a lot of shelter, although it had no perspex window. That was beyond my DIY capabilities. She was a wet wee boat.

34 Seònaid and AMF, both sober—honest!

We headed off to Soay as I had read Gavin Maxwell and Tex Geddes books and carried a special message from Bill Willis[1] to Tex. Bill and Tex had been buddies in the fishing game. The mooring harbour facing Skye becomes a pool at low spring tides, just like the inner harbour in Port Ramsay, Lismore, and it's best to enter on a rising tide.

I was aggressively chased in by a fishing boat that nearly ran us down; I guessed it belonged to Tex, who did not like strangers. Seònaid was enraged and spitting sparks but I said, 'Just leave it. I'll get him.'

Circling round his stern, I shouted, 'Can I pick up a spare mooring, as an easterly gale is forecast?'

'Certainly not. These are fishermen's moorings.'

Seònaid has now sharpened a knife and is intent on boarding the opposition. Again, I circled, 'Bill Willis says he's better-looking, a better fisherman and can drink more whisky than you,' and dropped the hook a bit further off with an '*Ist, ist, bi samhach,*'[2] to Seònaid. 'He'll come.'

He did, full of insults about me, my yacht and my rubber dinghy.

'How much did that cost?' prodding my dinghy with an oar.

'£600 at Nancy Blacks.' This was 30 years ago.

'I got mine for twenty.'

'I can see that. It's full of bloody holes,' and then kept speaking Gaelic to Seònaid, as I knew he did not have any.

I then offered him tea or coffee and said I had heard he had been banned from Mallaig for being too frisky. He came aboard and proved to be a very interesting and complex chap; he was very ahead of his time in trying to grow lobsters in tanks. We were stormbound for two or three days and were invited round to his house for tea and cake, which was just as well, as we were down to our last packet of oatcakes.

We then jumped over to Canna, as I thought the wind was going into the west and Canna is bombproof in a westerly. Unfortunately, the wind blew like stink from the east again, so we hung on our two anchors as Sanday is flat and gives no shelter. By the time we got ashore we were eating something from the bottom of a locker.

Some loon kept trying to anchor ahead of us but of course kept blowing back towards us; he was 40 feet and we were 22 feet. As Canna is bad for

---

[1] stories about my friend Bill could fill another book
[2] Hush, hush, be quiet.

Dunfillin

35 Ruadh The family said he was thick but I said he was a free spirit.

holding due to the *slat-mhara*[3] I kept shouting, 'use an angel' as the anchor was too small for 40 feet. An angel is any weight halfway down the anchor chain to give you more grip on the bottom. He took no heed, or maybe he thought I was referring to that heavenly body with wings.

Seònaid lashed the rubber boat on our bow to act as a fender, but he missed us by a few feet, shouting, 'Tickety boo! The fisherman laddie will give us a tow.' He was dressed rather fetchingly in a green shooting jacket and yellow wellies. 'Lord,' I thought, 'these were the chappies who with nothing but a revolver and a swagger stick strode forward to give the Hun a good thrashing.' Rule Britannia! I think that Seònaid is mentally (but not too much) like me and physically like my mother with her auburn hair and flashing eyes when her blood is up.

One night, out with Ruadh, our Irish setter, we were attacked by a huge mastiff, so Seònaid grabbed his collar and punched him in the nose till he ran away—good gear in sma' bodies.

I told the children that Auntie Seòna was once dropped into enemy territory on a parachute with a knife, a gun and a bottle of whisky. On the way down she had a few slugs and on landing shot a couple of the opposition and dispatched the rest with the knife.

---

[3] seaweed (tangle or oarweed)

What is the moral of this tale, children? Don't upset Auntie Seòna when she has a drink in her! Seònaid qualified as a lawyer and then trained as a teacher. After a few years in Japan she is now a Special Education teacher in the Northern Territory, Oz. I take my hat off to her and wish I had her guts.

36 Seònaid MacDonald, my daughter (2010)

FIONN

Setting out from Dysart in *Fraoch Eilean*[1], a Hurley-20 and my first yacht, I had Fionn (7) and a friend who was good on a hill, but not in a boat. *Fraoch Eilean* was really a big skiff with a lid and had an enormous red jib that would have done on a 30-foot craft. Once it was up and pulling, I just held on. It was a lovely day, and so with the sun in the heavens and joy in my heart, I set off from Fife towards Edinburgh.

At first there were a lot of boats about, but as the sky began to darken, they disappeared one by one. Time to get back to Dysart, I told the crew, but as we approached the harbour I realised, with that sinking feeling, that Dysart was tidal and the tide was out. I had been used to deep water harbours on the west of Scotland. Ach well, off to Kirkcaldy against wind and ebb. The bilge-keeled 20-foot pointed like a barge and then I fouled a lobster pot with a bloody milk carton as a pickup buoy.

Ranting about east coast fishermen too mean to buy proper buoys, I got the 4HP Seagull on aboard and by the time I had sorted this mess out I was off Dysart again. Should I drop the hook and wait for the tide to turn? The wind was rising and the light fading, so it was a run to Methil. This was intended as a wee sail round the bay and I had nothing aboard except a handheld compass, not even a roadmap. I only knew the pubs in Methil and had never been into the harbour by boat; I knew if I missed it, it was the North Sea, and my chances of making Norway were not good. Placing Fionn in the companionway within reach and giving him a large supply of chocolate, I headed east. The rudder started to slip (I found later that it was fastened with a screw) and then the jib blew out. Oh, Lordy, Lordy, this is serious and the wee boy with me.

---

[1] heather island

I managed to get the jib down and tied, so then it was main but the rudder was slipping and could not be relied on to tack. Better get this right, *a laochain*[2]. I was now roaring along in the dark under full main. I had my teeth so firmly clenched that slivers of enamel were flying off. I thought of deliberately putting her ashore when I saw the lights of Methil and roared up the fairway like a scalded cat. Suddenly it was like heaven on earth and I could breathe again.

My Polish friend Vakmer Klinki and my wife Diane were waiting for us in Dysart. Vakmer had said to Diane when we did not appear for tea that, 'Lachlan don't know much about sailing yet, but he knows a bit about the sea and will make for Methil.' This did not put Fionn off and he is now on his own second yacht down in Brixham on the south coast of England.

Vakmer suggested we take the boat back to Dysart the following day although the wind was still strong. We were working our way out of the long fairway in Methil with the wind on the nose as tacking was out and the 4HP Seagull was labouring. The prop kept coming out of the water, so I stood behind Vakmer on the afterhatch and held on to the stern stay which put the prop a little deeper and gave it more bite. It was like riding a bucking bronco and then the bold boy said, 'Have you got a free hand?' 'Not really,' I said, holding on like grim death. 'Why?'

'I can't see where we are going. My specs have got salted up with the spray. Can you give them a wipe?'

'Get this boat back to Methil, you mad Polish bastard!'

Vakmer laughed and we went back and waited for a week. A lovely man who used to weep when in his cups and talking about the war. Lovely people, the Poles, and great friends of ours when things were bad.

§§§§§

---

[2] little hero

37 Fionn, my son, and AMF

Fionn joined the Metropolitan Police as a cadet at 18 years old. I used to visit down in his Met Police section house in London and one Sunday morning we went for a stroll. An eye-catching lady was speaking to a group of people, so I engaged her in conversation and she asked us to join them for a spot of gospel singing. It was terrific! As the choir swung, the band rocked and I got excited and entered mentally into the whole scene.

It got better. People came out shouting, 'Ah's done drink, ah's done drugs,' and then fainted. Excitement mounted and I started to shake, thinking, I'll run up and shout, 'I've done drink, I've done drugs, and I've done eightsome reels.' What the hell, *Lachainn!* Strike a blow for the Hielans!

Fionn leaned over and whispered in my ear, 'Don't even think about it, Father.' That boy can read me like a book.

§§§§§

38 Fionn, Diane and Kären
Diane says we have been married, on and off, for 55 years!

Fionn and his wife Kären did 30 years in the police. Kären got the Queen's Police Medal for working with young people and Fionn ended up an inspector, has now done an MA and is studying to be a marine surveyor. Brine in the blood!

KÄREN'S FIRST SAIL

My son Fionn and his then-girlfriend Kären were courting. She was not used to small boats and her boat-christening was first with the Hurley 22 *Salvo* and then with *An t-Each* (the Horse).

A CalMac ferry was approaching us, leaving a big wake and I said to Fionn to wait until the ferry was past and go in hard to the swell and give Kären a shoogle. I went up to the bow and was cavorting about when we shot into the biggest wave. The 22 was low, with a sharp bow and not a lot of free board. I saw what was happening and jumped up holding on to the fore-stay, my timing was out and I came down as the wave came up … to my waist. Kären was lying in the scuppers, helpless with laughter, so I went to my bunk in the huff.

I had just bought the Centaur from an East Coast fisherman who assured me that, *'if she taaks mair than a cupful o' waater in a season,'* he would be most surprised (but he had never had the sails up and used her as a motorboat). The engine gleamed but the rest was dodgy!

We were between Lady's Rock and Lismore lighthouse in a stiff south-easterly breeze on the jib and engine, when the jib slackened and the engine stopped. I said to myself, 'no problem, I'll get up the main.' No luck there: the previous owner had fitted cheap Heath Robinson style lazy jacks, which prevented the sail going up; Lismore rocks loomed large. 'Any island but Lismore.' The thought flashed through my mind as a I raced aft, putting my foot through the rotten spray hood. Kären's eyes grew larger. I managed to get some sail up and clawed my way off, started the engine and headed to Dunstaffnage and repairs.

39 Lismore Lighthouse

Heading into the harbour at full throttle, the engine jammed in full ahead. Kären courageously was in the bows by now, clutching the boat hook ready to help. The boat hook had been made for me by a chum who worked in Weirs of Cathcart and he seemed to have become mixed up between a boat hook and a Lochaber axe, a formidable weapon. The onlookers on the shore thought they were witnessing the return of the Vikings and fled the pontoon we were aiming at.

What an introduction to sailing for Kären. I see now why she was given the Queen's Police Medal at work for her staying power and for working with young people. She still comes with us sailing now and then, and I wonder why. It must be love!

GRANDCHILDREN

This is good, because I did not have any grandparents; they were all dead. I'm glad we had our children early, as this gives time for their children. Brianna is studying architecture, Isobel is sitting her A-Levels, Euan is in high school and they are all lovely.

40 Isobel, Brianna and Euan

41 The Hairy MacDonalds: Issy, Euan, Kären, Fionn and Brianna

CARS

My first car was a Hillman Minx with lots of chrome, and cost £250 in 1966, the year I qualified. I had failed the test a couple of times and my doc said he'd give me a couple of pills 'to slow you down'. I told him I did not take drugs, took the afternoon off work, had two or three large vodkas, and sailed through it. The instructor said I was more relaxed this time! I did not think of whisky and spirits as drugs till I came to AA.

It had four good radials and a duff spare (cross-ply), so when I had a puncture and put on the spare the first wet day, I lost it and most of the chrome on the starboard-side on a lamppost.

Over 65 mph there was a burning smell, and going on a trip to Cornwall, I cut a hole in the dash to insert a radio, but then found that you could either start the car or the radio, but not both together. This was the only car I really loved.

I lost interest in cars after that, and in Fife my chum Derek, who worked in a Mazda garage, would change them now and again. Up in Lismore on holiday, I had him change the car without seeing the new one. I only knew that it was a white Mazda with four doors and a low mileage. Derek said that he had never done a deal like this before.

The only new cars I ever bought were two Fords. The 2-litre white Capri had a long bonnet and a small racing-type steering wheel and made 'vroom vroom' noises when you pulled the throttle. I lost it going through Rannoch Moor early one morning, hit the bank and landed back on the straight road and bounced a few times. The undercarriage was never right after that, so I sold it.

The Ford Cortina was bought simply because it was blue and I could instantly—with white tape—turn it into a Scottish flag, fore and aft. Those were the days, when you could hear Fordies trying to start on cold mornings and men across the county drying the plugs in the oven. Quick Start was sold by the gallon and heart attacks and blood pressure soared as punters tried to jump start them down hills. I just abandoned mine at the side of the road and caught a bus.

The cars did not return the mileage quoted, as I knew they tested them with no seats, down a hill and driven by a small monkey.

Derek my friend sold me an overpriced banger, and when I remarked on that fact, he said, 'Weel, Lachie, you were going to get ripped off anyway, and is it not better to be done by a friend than a stranger?'

My son sold me his BMW, but it had rear-wheel drive and skidded, so I really gave it away and was strangely sad. Seònaid's Welsh friend said it was a classic, so I wrote a poem about it (see below) and bought her lunch.

I had a lovely wee Jap with a Merc engine which did 60 mpg but sold it and brought a Volvo with an engine you could plough fields with. Fionn said that fewer people die in them than any other model. Diane always wanted one and the truth is that I started counting up the money I have spent on boats, and guilt got the better of me.

If I ever win the pools, which is difficult as I don't do them, the first thing I'll get is a chauffeur, or even a chauffeuse!

The Beamer

A poem written on the demise of an old car

The Cult Classic you were called by a Welsh chum of Seòna's,
Perhaps a trifle premature
You served the family well and Fionn petted you like a child
We just used you like a car—black, square and powerful
But I was sad to see you go—
Left in the forecourt like an abandoned child

DOCS AND HOSPITALS

I was about ten years old when the doctor came to call. He said I was eating too much bear honey, gave me pills and put me on a milk diet. A fortnight later, he gave me more pills and said to give me the run of the house. I thought the expression was very funny.

A fortnight later, he said to my mother I was OK, just dodging school. The next day I fainted, they took me to the mainland and removed my appendix! The general consensus was that the local doctor was good at broken bones and sewing people up, but his diagnostic skills left much to be desired.

In the hospital, I was the only child in a large ward full of men. The day after the operation, the nurse gave me castor oil for my bowels. The effect of it hit me like a hammer about lunchtime, and despite pressing the bell till my thumb bled, she was too late. I managed to contain it in my pyjama bottoms, tied up the legs and handed it out to the nurse who marched down the ward holding it in front of her like a steaming dumpling. The ward cheered, and I hid under the bedclothes for the rest of the day.

Events on the accident front fell quiet for a few years, apart from missing my femoral artery by an inch or two with a Bowie knife, leaving a crescent shaped scar. This has been handy over the years for entertaining children. You paint the scar with lipstick, paint eyes above it, flex the muscle then tell the kids that you can throw your voice and sing 'Swanee River'. I bill it as The Singing Knee. For adults, you say it was due to a sabre duel, Class of 66; he was small, but vicious.

There are various editions of this next incident, but I prefer this one. I can remember saying to a man on the platform of a Dundee bus, 'I never hit a man with glasses', whereupon he took them off, put them in his pocket and hit me on the chin. I took off like a rocket. The bus was doing about 30 mph. I was told later that I hit a bus queue and the punters went up in the air like skittles. I discovered I was still mobile, although my right arm was not under control. I legged it round the back streets to the Dundee Royal Infirmary, where a friend's fiancée was working as the admissions officer. What happened to patient confidentiality? She later told my girlfriend that I was chased around Admissions by nurses, and wouldn't take my clothes off for any of them. This was not like me; I must really have been out of it!

My arm was in and out of plaster for about six months, during which time I failed my finals and got married—the two are not connected—and found a job labouring at Loch Awe to finance my winter exams (a case of Merry Christmas and Happy Resits!).[1]

Quite some years later, I landed in the Southern General Hospital in Glasgow, tired and depressed with nervous debility—well that's what the doctor called it anyway. I believe it was overindulgence in *uisge beatha*, the water of life—or death for some. I met old Jean there who fell in love with me; I was 43, and she was 83. She said I had been mixing with the wrong kind of people who had led me astray, to which I readily agreed, although no-one else did.

Another younger female patient whom I thought was allowed the freedom of going into town led me a merry dance on a manic tour of the shops. I found out later that she was a sectioned patient and should not have been out of the hospital at all. Oh boy, can I find them!

A lump in my groin, a cancer scare and varicose veins: all left me in and out of hospitals enjoying the pre-meds. 'Yes, Nurse, I need a pre-med—a large one, please. It's the nearest thing I can get to a bottle of champagne these days!'

On Boxing Day 1988, after a hearty breakfast of ham and eggs and two fags, I had a heart attack. Bent over with pain, I announced to the family, still lounging about in dressing gowns, that this was not a gag. After a couple of days in the hospital, I discovered I could set off the monitor by raising my blood pressure thinking of things that irritated me. Sussed out by a dragon-faced sister, I was banished to a side room where the gale from the (NHS) window blew over my Get Well cards. Out of hospital after ten days, I kept off fags by smoking herbal weeds (not wacky baccy), which raised blisters on my tongue.

There was no improvement, so I was given a quadruple bypass from a chap whose initials were JC. Failing to raise a smile by remarking that with

---

[1] This is Diane's gag and she wants to keep it!

initials like that I was in good hands, and I wanted him early to bed that night with a glass of hot milk, I thought, 'stop digging.'

After a week, he said, did I want to go home, and I said no thanks. The decor and food were much better here than at home (cheeky monkey—Diane), so he kept me another week. I was on BUPA that time.

As for the lump in my groin, I was nervous at the thought of operations to the family jewels area. I was dissuaded against putting an indelible ink line with 'cut here' at the operation site by my wife, just in case the surgeon did not have a sense of humour.

As it turned out, she was right. I convinced the nurse to give me a large pre-med and was in great form as they wheeled me into the operating theatre. After entertaining porters and nurses to a few groin gags, I was well into that old World War II favourite to the tune of 'Colonel Bogey's March':

> Hitler has only got one ball,
> Goring had two but they were small,
> Himmler had something similar,
> But poor Goebbels had no balls at all.

When the anaesthetists and the surgeon came in muttering about turning his theatre into a music hall, it was then a case of 'wham, bam, thank you Ma'am, with the gas and I was *oot the game*, as they say.

The latest is that they wanted to give me new knees (years of praying), but I put off the evil hour. When I was young, lots of people died in hospital, but medics are getting better at it, and if you find both the surgeon and the anaesthetist sober on the same day, you're home and dry!

I know people who are terrified of general anaesthetics, but I have had so many it doesn't bother me much. For many, it is the fear of dying under the anaesthetic. As one of my professors used to say, 'There are four levels: awake, light dental anaesthesia, deep surgical anaesthesia, and death.'

DRINK—OR LONG DISTANCE DENIAL

New shock horror: the powers that be have discovered that the Scots drink too much. Does the Pope have a balcony?

For goodness' sake, the Romans wrote that the Celts drank to excess, never watered their wine, and *pit the heid* on people who upset them—what's new? Many young people experiment with tobacco, drink and drugs, and a small percentage get hooked.

When I was young, whisky was used as a social lubricant, and also as a medicine; after all the Gaelic for whisky is *uisge beatha:* water of life. You were given a toddy for a cold, and butter honey and whisky balls for a sore throat. Older people knew of the dangers of drink, but for the young it was a rite of passage to get a few drinks in before the dance. This did not lead to great problems as we were poor; alcohol was expensive and you burned off the effect after a couple of square dances. Social control was also strong on the island and if you showed the effects of alcohol at the dances you were quietly taken outside and sent home.

Physically, all drugs are cleared from the system after a couple of weeks' abstinence, so instead of keeping people in clinics for weeks and months with the state paying for it, give them two to three weeks and double the number of people going through the system. This gives enough time to detox and establish two principles:

1. no drink or drugs
2. the start of a twelve-step programme; the gateway to recovery for many people.

The word alcoholic is thrown about with gay abandon these days. Dylan Thomas said, 'An alcoholic is someone you don't like who drinks as much as you do!'

I drank to drown my sorrows but the b******s learned to swim! The best definition of alcoholism I have heard is that it is a primary chronic disease that manifests itself physically, mentally and spiritually.

My own alcoholism is contained one day at a time by AA principles. My other disease, depression, comes unannounced like a thief in the night and shuts off the lights to the power source. I stop meetings, prayer and avoid AA literature and discussion. If AA is God-driven, is depression Devil-driven? The words devil, bad, evil are not popular these days—nor indeed politically correct (PC)—but if PC-ness is linguistic fascism, then get rid of it.

If some human beings are hard-wired to violence and greed, and indeed, if social control is breaking down, then we must stop half-baked legislation and pussy-footing around. It would appear that respect for truth, family life, honesty, men and women of the cloth and capable politicians are in terminal decline.

Trendy leftism has failed; let's try good old-fashioned common sense again.

Denial

He has the haunted washed-out look of the long-distance drunk;
Overwork, death in the family, misfortune—
What is the excuse this time?
Denial is in his very bones and time is running out;
The bloodshot eyes have the cunning flicker of a cornered animal.

PLOYS

After World War II, with no television or internet, we made our own amusement, and as well as ceilidhs and dances, fishing and fornication, we played a lot of jokes on each other.

§§§§§

At the Glasgow Fair[1], the local girls, many of whom trained as nurses in Glasgow, brought their girlfriends home to the island. On the first night they were there, and to get a better view of the ladies, some lads would put a clod of earth over the chimney top. The occupants would stagger out coughing and crying; relationships were often struck up. It did not work at our house, as Father leapt out with the old twelve-bore and fired a couple of shots in the air. No romance that night!

§§§§§

We loved April Fool's Day and got up to some complicated plots. A good one was to get someone to carry a letter to another house—the further away the better—with the sealed message: 'Do not laugh and do not smile, but send the gowk another mile!' It's no wonder we were fit.

§§§§§

Sweets and chocolate were scarce after the war, but I acquired a square of chocolate laxative. A tiny piece would do the trick, but I broke the bar in half and gave them to a couple of kids who were not at the top of my friendship

---

[1] local holiday which takes place in the last two weeks of July

list. They staggered into school the following day, ashen and pale. 'It was him!' they said, pointing at me!

§§§§§

I loved comics, and I got this gag from *Oor Wullie*. Cover the underside with thick mustard and encourage the victim to take a bite out of the tea/digestive biscuit. A neighbour was working under a car, and I persuaded him to take a bite. Reluctantly he did, and I rammed the lot down his throat and fled. Thinking I had gone far enough, I was rolling about holding myself with glee when the whole world exploded. He caught up with me and rubbed the remainder of the mustard into my eyebrows; the tears ran down my face for a long time.

§§§§§

Creamola Foam came in tins and was flavoured (only lemon in those days) bicarbonate of soda with sugar. You were supposed to mix a spoonful with water and it foamed up to give a fizzy drink, even if it did leave an aftertaste of bicarb. We loved it and it was a convenient drink as you could make it up from a small tin, so transporting it to the island was not a problem. A friend once put some into her auntie's po-po[2] which she used every night for huge streamies which wakened us all up. As soon as the warm urine hit the powder it foamed up over the rim and the kids in the house dissolved in laughter hearing poor Auntie crying, 'Get the doctor, get the doctor, quick, quick! I'm dying!' shouted in Gaelic, of course.

§§§§§

The darkness at Halloween and the fear of ghosts made this a rich time for frightening yourself and other people. In the dark alone, and going home, I spun as I ran, because everyone knew that the *bòcain*[3] came at you from the back.

---

[2] pee-pot (chanty/chamber pot)
[3] ghosts

§§§§§

St Valentine's Day was excellent for sending cards to unlikely recipients with the sender's origin, clumsily disguised, especially if they were straight-laced elderly folk, for example:

> I love you a little, I love you aw' mighty,
> I wish your pyjamas were close to my nightie.
> Don't be mistaken, and don't be misled;
> I mean on the clothesline, and not in the bed.

§§§§§

Some gags, like the lighted paper in the urinal trough, were terrific. In old school lavs, a running trough of water passed under the cubicles and a lighted ball of paper released at the top end got a succession of screams.

§§§§§

Sailing with a friend in the Utter Hebrides, he discovered an old birds' nest in the back of our rope tidy in the cockpit and wrongly blamed me for not cleaning up well enough. Every time I was ashore during the next week, I put kippers, socks, underpants in the same place, but finally, a litre of Bacardi rum—he had suffered enough.

§§§§§

Sometimes in the honesty box where you leave money for tying up your boat for the night on the pier, I would leave a £5 note, with a pal's boat's name on it saying, 'Due to recent financial circumstances, this is all I can afford.' He, of course, had not been there for months. He never mentioned it to me but I know he had his suspicions.

§§§§§

Another sailing chum used to move up to the bow of the boat with the *Guardian* newspaper and a roll of toilet paper. He wedged himself with his bum sticking out over the water (a type of bidet), and seemed to stay there a long time, reading. One trip, I had the shotgun with me and, waiting till he was settled in and the boat goose-winging, fired both barrels in the air. He ended up trousers still down, with both arms and legs wrapped round the mast, and the *Guardian* in a watery grave.

§§§§§

Laughter seriously improves your health.

THE SAYINGS OF GRANNIE BROCHAN (CONFUCIUS OF THE WEST)

I can see her yet: the mutch, the black dress, the green-eyed cat sitting on her lap, and the half bottle in her apron pocket.

§§§§§

The mother of parliaments, *mo thòn*[1]. More like the *hoor* of Westminster.

§§§§§

Life is like a sewer: what you get out of it depends on what you put into it.

§§§§§

If your swingin' on both anchors, it doubles your chance of a date on a Saturday night.

§§§§§

Those that mind don't matter, and those that matter don't mind.

§§§§§

On failing to recognise a word, '*pass that yin ower dattie*[2], that'll be Latin.'

§§§§§

---

[1] my backside
[2] daughter

Try everything in life, apart from incest and Morris dancing.[3]

§§§§§

After a spell of good weather: 'Mark my words: we'll suffer for this.' Calvin rules, ya bass.

§§§§§

'Get off the stove, Grandma. You're too old to be riding the range.' Grannie was not too proud to make fun of herself!

§§§§§

Modern poetry is prose that does not reach the side of the page.

§§§§§

Taking a foolscap paper down to two or three sentences is called a précis; the reverse is called bullshit.

§§§§§

If you really hate a man, give him an old wooden boat as a present.[4]

§§§§§

With Grannie, as English gained traction, speaking about a smart chap: '*Chan eil e* slack, *tha e* tight—*'s e clipper a th' ann.*' And on seeing a fast craft going up the loch: '*Chunnaic mi* motorboat *a' dol suas an loch le* speed bloody.'

§§§§§

I am a subject but I'd rather be a citizen.
§§§§§
After a big meal: '*Nae mair, ahm ful tae the paste beads.*' Translation for when in polite company: 'No more, thank you. One more bite—even a morsel—would be an overindulgence.

---

[3] she may have picked this up elsewhere!
[4] This one has really come back to haunt me.

§§§§§

Lies, damned lies, statistics … and audits!

§§§§§

(That's enough. You're fired!—Ed)

GLOBAL WARMING AND CLIMATE CHANGE

'The time has come,' the Walrus said, 'To talk of many things:'[1]

New shock horror: global warming, climate change, ozone layer, CO_2 in emissions, floods, conservation, recycling, carbon footprint and so on. All doom and gloom; it's locust time again. *Those whom the gods want to destroy, they first make mad.*[2] But it is a good line: frighten the proletariat out of their minds and then control them. None of this is of course new to us from the Highlands and Islands. They used to keep us quiet with Clearances; now it's Armageddon.

On my island over the years, we have used fish oil, paraffin, coal, wood, peat, and then Calor gas and finally electricity to provide us with energy. The *crùisgeanan* (fish oil lamps), were used up to a hundred years ago, as they had been for thousands of years. There was little peat on Lismore, and with the advent of commercial lime quarries, that wood was soon used up, and we had to get timber and peat from Morvern and Benderloch. Up until the Second World War, old ladies on the island turned the *buachar mairt* (cow dung) over to dry and used it as fuel. Before we had Calor gas in the 1950s and electricity in the 1970s, we used paraffin for cooking and lighting. We had simple oil lamps, tilly lamps and aladdin lamps, which Father filled, cleaned and trimmed regularly, as he had done as a boy at sea.

I had discovered girls, drink, dancing and creeping in late at night, trying to avoid steps number three and seven, which creaked—CREAK—dammit—it was *four* and seven. Mother's voice rang out sleepily, '*An e sin do

---

[1] Lewis Carroll 1832–98 English writer and logician: *Through the Looking-Glass* (1872) ch. 4
[2] ancient proverb (anon)

fhèin, a Lachuinn?' (Is that you, Lachlan?), avoiding the obvious smart reply of, 'No, it's the Boston Strangler,' I would assure her all was well.

I certainly did not want Mother up, as she could smell women and drink at forty paces. Father could and did sleep through an earthquake. Into bed fast; hell, I need a pee, so back down for a Jimmy Riddle, and more creaking. Now she's awake.

'Are you OK?'

'Yes, yes, yes.'

Just back to bed, and I need another one; now it's a psychological problem. If I go down again, she's up and she'll smell women, drink and eightsome reels. What to do? I cannot pee out of the skylight, as I'm not that well-endowed and I don't have enough pressure in my bladder to reach three feet above my head. Salvation, I see the big paraffin lamp. It's half empty, and I fill it—bliss!

In the morning, I had forgotten the problems of the night before, and that evening, as Father attempted to light the lamp and was rewarded with acrid, black, smelly smoke, I exit smartly stage left to the roars of, 'that bloody cat's peed in the lamp!'

§§§§§

A family of four in the 1950s used a tenth of the energy we use today. There were two cars, a couple of tractors and a lorry on the island until the 1940s, and we still had horses' ploughing matches until 1950. Shanks's pony and bicycles ruled. We covered long distances by jogging and walking, as our forefathers did in peace and war.

My uncle John from America was the first to use artificial fertiliser in his garden, and had big beautiful fruit and veg. As neighbours praised the size of his carrots and onions, mother would say, '*Tha fhios am, ach chan eil blas idir orra.*' (I see that, but they have no taste).

When we got a Seagull 4HP outboard, we motored into the wind to the fishing grounds, fished and rowed home with the wind behind us. After the Second World War, the drift nets went out of fashion, and in came the seine and the purse nets, followed by the echo sounder and fish finders.

My uncle Jock in Port Ramsay went in for whelks big time during and after the war, when his boat the *Lady Margaret* was laid up. He collected them in clean water, well away from habitation, and never took them unless there was an R in the month. Then, it was off to the market post haste. Now they are collected all year round, left exposed at half-tide, for days on end, near marinas and sewage outlets. Whelks are not particular where their food comes from, nor of what they have to nourish them!

42 The *Lady Margaret* at Port Ramsay. The last of the Scottish working sail boats, her last voyage was 50 tons of coal for Lismore Lighthouse on 20 June 1939, five days after I was born.[3]

---

[3] The house at the end belonged to MacDonalds who were boatbuilders there in the 1930s and related to us. They moved to Oban and had Port Beag near the lighthouse pier, just beside where the lifeboat is moored nowadays. They built a rowing boat for my father in the 1930s and another for him in the 1950s. I believe they moved to New Zealand. Jock was the last to row in that particular fashion: straight back and short strokes, the only way one can tow a big boat with a hawser. I am grateful to Duncan Black, Port Ramsay, for this information.

The first time I heard the word conservation was in connection with filling teeth at dental college and recycling was getting home on your bicycle after you had been to see your girl.

During and after the war, everything was used and reused: nails, bits of wood, old bedsteads for gates, parachute silk for undies, gas bags for school bags, and when you put your elbows through your woolly jersey, the sleeves were unpicked and you had a pullover, then depending on where the holes appeared you had a tank top, and later your jersey was reduced to making socks and mittens.

The local newspaper, *The Oban Times,* was a case in point for recycling. We bought it and read it, used it first as a tablecloth, lining shelves, and in cutting it into shapes to amuse the children, then for firelighters, also crumpling some of it to dry out boots and shoes, and using it as wrapping paper, cutting it into squares and finally hang it on a string in the little shed at the bottom of the garden; now you were really talking recycling.

A carbon footprint was new also. Miners had carbon footprints alright; they died in their own phlegm, Miners' Lung it was called, like somehow it was their own fault. We used little carbon, since we did not travel far, only Oban or Fort William, and travelling to Glasgow was a very big deal. 'Remember to change your drawers, Lan, if you're going to Oban, we don't want you to get run over, land in the hospital and give the family a bad name!'

Over the past two hundred years, the First World has burned millions of tons of carbon fuels. Surely the First World cannot say to the Second and Third Worlds, 'Don't do as I do.' Why not? The First World decides who is rich or poor, who lives or dies, has nuclear fuel, clean water and a future for their children.

Nowadays, my family regularly travel to Australia, Japan, the USA and other far-flung places. They are all interesting, but I have seen as much beauty and had as much fun in a radius of ten miles around my birthplace.

HATCHES, MATCHES AND DISPATCHES

Over in the Bahamas, they had an early morning television programme called *Sunrise, Midday and Sunset*, which is the equivalent of our 'hatches, matches and dispatches', and I think is rather classier than our phrase, which seems to have been dreamt up in an effort not to take birth, marriage and death too seriously. My late cousin Colin, who was a commissioner out there, thought the Bahamian phrase was rather naff, but then he was not such a sensitive soul as I.

As a child, weddings and funerals made a big impression, but I cannot remember being at a christening, not even my own. I suppose the reason for that is that few children were born around that time, and being a Protestant island, no big deal was made of christenings.

Births and Christenings

My own children, born two years apart, were christened together, the reasons for this being:

1. we were up from England on holiday (where I was 'practising' my newly-qualified profession of dentistry) and wanted to get them christened in the proper fashion in Scotland
2. my wife's father was a first-class organist, and his minister was called MacDonald
3. it was free.

We promised to bring them up in the faith, but don't seem to have made a very good job of it since they only go to church on the big occasions: the hatches, matches and dispatches yet again. I've told them not to worry since I will put in a good word for them at the Pearly Gates.

43 Seònaid and Fionn

Weddings

Personally, I enjoy weddings best, and have been to quickies, long-distance events and even marathons. One day in Glasgow, just passing on the street with my wife, we were asked to be witnesses to a poor young pair of wee souls who were on the run from her deranged family. She could not run fast since she was eight months pregnant. We said 'of course' and tried to help this skint pair by buying them a wedding meal and seeing them off to Inverness, with a merry, quip of: 'drop in and see us sometime', forgetting our address was there, engraved for ever more on their wedding certificate.

Two weeks later, they turned up on our doorstep and stayed for a long time. At this point, they had no money, no job and nowhere to stay. We tried to help, but not long after the police were round at our door to pick them up for pinching a cardigan from an old lady, and stealing from the hotel where the man had found work using my name as a reference. We were very naive in those days.

§§§§§

I was hugely honoured and touched when my son asked me to be his best man when he was married in Somerset a few years ago. The Scottish tartan contingent added a bit of colour to a lovely day in this green and pleasant land. Diane's cousin Thorfinn from Orkney, a splendid fellow who could play the pipes, supplied the music.

My speech was directed mainly at my son, as I knew his chums would appreciate it, even if he didn't. It went like this:

'The sports master phoned to say that Fionn urinated in the pool that day:
"Wee boys often do that."
"But not from the top board."'
or
'An irate father came to the door saying that Fionn and his daughter were playing doctors and nurses.
"Seven year old children often play like that."
"But he took her appendix out."'
Great fun among the working class!

§§§§§

44 Our wedding day at St Andrews University Chapel Jock Linton, Me, Diane, Omy
(note the arm in plaster)

I was married with my arm in plaster and my niece was married in a castle, but the wedding that really took my fancy and on which I have dined out for several years was of an old university chum whose son was married in a ruined, haunted church in Argyllshire.

My grandfather used to tell of Lismore weddings in his youth, when the reception was in a big barn and the two opposing teams were fed facing each other at long trestle tables. These weddings lasted a long time, and the overexcited guests, becoming more tired and confused, would commence fighting and throwing boiled fowls and pats of butter at each other. This is one wedding which could compete with the best of the stories. Let me paint a picture.

The groom's retinue, of which I was one, were beautifully dressed in full Highland gear and were walking, I must admit, with a bit of a swagger (which makes your kilt swing with a carefree, cocky air) as befits the descendants of a Highland gentleman. At the risk of sounding like a Mrs Bouquet (or Bucket) straight from television's *Keeping Up Appearances*, the bride's mob came from the Lowlands and appeared to be clad in charity shop frocks (the women, that is). The men were in dusty grey outfits which looked suspiciously like demob suits.

The day started well, but tension was mounting. The groom's brother arrived late, drunk and on a high-powered motorbike. He found the whole occasion of his brother being married hugely amusing and kept making ribald comments from the back of the ruined kirk. There were certain shades of Burns's *Tam o' Shanter* here,

> *There sat auld Nick, in shape o' beast;*
> *A towzie tyke, black, grim, and large,*
> *To gie them music was his charge:*
> *He scre'd the pipes and gart them skirl,*
> *Till roof and rafters a' did dirl.*
> *Coffins stood round, like open presses,*
> *That shaw'd the dead in their last dresses;*

Later we retired to a nearby hall for refreshments and fun! The food was in abundance and consisted mainly of fish, as the groom's father had access to the local fish farm. The day was hot, the band was well primed, and the hordes spilled out into the car park and surrounding countryside to have room to dance those old favourites: Strip the Wimmen and Dashing White Sergeant (so un-PC). Mind-altering substances of both liquid and powder were in abundance and a sense of abandonment filled the air. I sat outside, waiting for Alice and the Mad Hatter to appear but they had not been invited—surreal, or what?

I had just finished singing (foul rumours were put about that this was what started the action), and had asked a lovely young girl to take a turn on the floor with me. But instead of taking my arm, she leapt onto the table and did a solo dance number (minus the pole). I must explain that by this time, the young lady mentioned had abandoned most of her clothes, apart from a mini-top and what appeared to be a diaphanous silk scarf round her hips. She had painted her face in a professional and rather attractive manner with a Saint Andrew's cross. Completing her performance to a rapturous round of applause (more than I had), she jumped down and was immediately punched in the face by a large woman from the other team. My companion, small but feisty, grabbed the microphone and made the announcement that, 'That fat, ugly, Lowland bitch punched me for no reason!'

Talk about the spark in the powder keg! All hell broke loose and the fighting began. It was like the bloody Wild West without revolvers.

Jumping into the fray, fists swinging, the best man asked me—one of the few people able to drive—to get rid of the women in the bridal party. Thankfully I obeyed orders.

I loaded the ladies into the people carrier, and was pulling away when my door was hauled open by a shirtless (it's the old Norse thing), bloodied member of the opposition. I thought, 'I need this like I need a hole in the head', but he addressed our semi-naked dancer and roared, in his best Pictish, *'Ye did bliddy richt girlie!'* Turning round without losing momentum, he smacked one of his own team in the chops. Tensions were rising in the opposition, but there was obviously justice here, too.

On reaching the home town at two in the morning, our dancer, whose eye was beginning to blacken and close, stopped the car, got out and said, 'I'm off to a party', and went casually along the street, not clad in much, but fortunately had retrieved her floppy brimmed hat with its large floral tributes attached, although by now it looked as though it had passed through the alimentary tract of an elephant.

I wondered aloud where the groom's father might be, but was told not to worry: he had stayed to take pictures of the fight. People think I make these stories up, but cross my heart, I don't need to—it's all true.

Who says Highland weddings were not what they used to be?

God bless them all!

Funerals

After World War II, when I was still quite small, women and children did not go to the graveside at a funeral, but stayed in the house. As time went by, the women went to church and then to the graveside, and then—the talk of the steamie[1]—a woman held one of the cords to lower in the casket! Recently at the funeral of a lifelong friend, all eight cords were held by women. I wanted to shout, 'Good on you gals. Who says women's lib has stalled? Now you can come too; grieve and freeze with the men' but felt that this would not be fitting from a sober and respected member of the community.

My father had good stories of funerals in days gone by. One time the whisky firkin was broached on the way to the church before the funeral, and they mislaid the coffin. The day was cold, the way was long, and the boys were weary; they laid the coffin down with reverence at the side of the road and decided to have a small refreshment or two. The discussion was of what a fine fellow the coffin occupant had been when living, and how noble he looked in death. But time was marching on, and refreshed physically, mentally and spiritually, the boys took off for the church minus the coffin.

§§§§§

The men traditionally walk behind on the way to the church. One icy day, my father fell and broke his arm. He always stressed that he did this on the way to the church, and not on the way back.

§§§§§

Another good Lismore custom, carried over from the days when people walked miles to and from the church, often in inclement weather, is that as you leave the graveyard, you are offered a choice of whisky, port, sherry, biscuits and lumps of cheese. Often there is a large amount left over, which gives the close family mourners a chance to grieve longer.

---

[1] public laundry

The Funeral

The deceased, a dear friend of mine, had married late for the second time. The widow asked me to say a few words and, as I left for the event, my wife handed me a poem which she said she had been keeping for my last trip! It was lovely, and painted the picture of the person leaving in the death craft, and all the people weeping or cheering as the case may be. No worries, however, as on the other side waited rellies and friends who had gone before, and they were laughing or booing as the case may be!

The team from the deceased's first marriage were there in large number, but there were only a few of us supporting the widow. It was a humanist funeral, and I had just finished my spiel when a daughter from the first marriage, who had not spoken to her father for years, burst onto the stage and delivered a speech that would have brought a tear to a glass eye, extolling the lovely relationship she had with her father.

At this, the latest widow exploded and demolished this hypocrite, ending with: although she had no children to the deceased, they had a lovely couple of wee dugs. Oh Lord, I thought, let me retain some measure of sanity here and bring the event to a close.

But no. The original wife/widow leapt to her feet and with a voice that would have wakened the dead, 'It's OK for you, you had him sober and I had him when he was a piss artist.' I was for the off, but the young widow insisted on staying to shake hands, which did not take long, as there was only half a dozen of our team left.

45 Dead Centre of Lismore

Knowing my deceased friend, I bet he was laughing and using his catchphrase of, 'Take it, but take it easy.'

I have just realised that after I have sung or spoken on at least three occasions, fighting broke out!

HOLIDAYS AND TRAVEL

Or 'Holy Days' as Grannie Brochan used to call them.
My grandparents had a holiday once—on the day they were married in Oban.

I was luckier than most of my peers, who only went to the Oban and Tobermory Highland Games. We had friends and rellies in Oban, Fort William, Glasgow and Edinburgh, so we went there for visits or overnight stays. Father, who was at sea most of his life, used to say, 'life is not worth a box of matches down in Glasgow', so nothing has changed.

In Oban, once I had got the ice-cream/sweets/sixpenny/balsa glider, the people and buildings rapidly gave me claustrophobia and I longed for the evening boat back to Lismore to get my shoes off and run—anywhere. Even as I speak today, I can still feel the soft, sensuous touch of the thick, green grass between my toes. My mother did not like me going barefoot outside because it reminded her of how poor some people were when she was young.

I think I started university in a holiday mood, majoring in girls and beer—that was a big mistake. When the end of the term exams came, my name was often absent from the pass list. The dangerous/odd thing was that I never learned from my mistakes. *Mañana, mañana*—there is no word in Gaelic to express such urgency! When God made time, he made a lot of it; but not for me. Life is not a rehearsal. The trouble with leaving things until the last minute is that they are often done badly—or not at all.

I suppose the three to four years I worked in England was a bit of a working holiday. Unfortunately, I spent most of it in a town which was like an upmarket sink estate with a steelworks at the centre of it. A bit of Central Scotland in the middle of England, but a diverse mix of people just the same. This was where I cut my teeth in dentistry and met interesting and exotic people.

This was in 1966 to 1970, and there were few ethnic minorities at that time. Our neighbours were mixed and lovely; a plumber from Aberdeen, a Latvian family from Riga and a Hell's Angel with one leg from the Forest of Dean ('there be queer folk in the Forest of Dean', so they say down there) and he was a dead ringer for Jesus. That is, of course, the white European image of Jesus. I felt strongly free and unshackled in England. Was I shaking off the bonds of John Knox, or the realisation that I had at last qualified and could feed my family?

Then came the Costa holidays; mainly in Spain (and Italy), one of the reasons being that in the late 1960s it was cheaper to holiday in Spain than stay at home. Sometimes we even came back home with money left over, and abroad you could become drunk for next to nothing. Looking at the UK city centres now, I can't remember half-naked women rolling about in the Spanish street or wet T-shirt competitions; they did that in the privacy of their own home!

In Italy we lost our son for a terrible, heart-stopping hour or so. His mother saw me coming down the beach and said to him, 'There's Daddy.' He ran off to meet me. A crowded beach, miles long, we passed each other by, unnoticed. He was only four years old, and must have walked for ages looking for me. Hundreds of hotels faced on to the beach, all looking very similar. We thought he could not possibly find his way back to our hotel. All of the staff, the guests and any other Italians on the beach went looking for him. There weren't so many redheaded children around on an Italian beach, and the Italians just loved children. Amazingly, he found his way back to the correct hotel. He found us, rather than we found him, so we had an idea that his future might be in the CID or similar!

At the risk of the Social Work Department coming after me, the horror of misplacing my son was equalled for a short time when my daughter slipped, or jumped, into a very deep outdoor pool where it was impossible to see the bottom. The time seemed endless as I felt around until I eventually got hold of her. She survived, and I aged ten years in a moment.

§§§§§

One of the best Costa holidays we had was with an Irish and Jewish couple that we met there. The Jewish couple came on the London flight with us, and that night, as we all sipped a small sherry in the bar, a very attractive, tall lady marched past, gripping her handbag in front of her. The bar was long and narrow, and at the end were glass sliding doors and three steps down to the swimming pool. The night was dark with no outside lights (another power cut). I had a premonition as she purposely marched through the glass doors, went down three steps and then there was a splash. As I headed for the pool myself, she appeared wet and bedraggled, back in the bar, still gripping her handbag in one hand, and a wet hairpiece in the other. She wordlessly marched back along the length of the bar spraying water in all directions.

My wife turned to me and said, 'she would be worth getting to know!' and she most certainly was the genuine article. This couple had just arrived from Dublin on the Aer Lingus flight which used to serve a fair amount of free booze. As the Irish couple appeared together half an hour later, we greeted them with cries of, 'encore, encore!'

The following evening the Jewish couple, my wife and myself were walking down a quiet street on the way out for a beer. Suddenly a car reversed out of a drive at speed, almost knocking two of us over. My new Jewish pal remonstrated loudly in his south London accent with the drunken Spanish driver. After swearing and threatening us in Spanish, the man drove off in a worse temper. A short time later, we were by then in a busier road, the open-topped car was cruising up and down, with our mad driver and another three big pals obviously looking for us!

'In here,' I shouted bravely, leaping down steps to a basement German bierkeller. Whilst the wives retreated to find a loo, my pal (all of 5 feet 4 inches or so) and I sat guarding the entrance to the club. I handed one of my heavy, wooden Scholl sandals to my wee pal and hoped we had not been seen by our Spanish Inquisition gangsters.

Nothing happened, so we relaxed and moved to a table. When it was time to stagger home, my sandals had disappeared from under the table. By the looks and laughter of the mainly Germanic audience, I guessed they had been nicked. Leaping to my feet I was well into a verse of 'Rule Britannia' when the rest dragged me to the door, to be met by two blonde Teutons, who seemed about seven feet tall. 'Oops,' I thought. 'The motormouth has done it again!'

'Very good Scottish joke,' said one German, and handed me back my sandals. How well the Gods looked after me.

One night I landed on my own in a bar with half-English, half-German patrons and, singing 'The Dam Busters March', bombed the German tables with peanuts. In the morning, the English crowd had gone and, standing at the bar at lunchtime with a wee refreshment and alone, a German chap came up and said, 'not so brave today, Scottie.' Exit stage left.

§§§§§

When the children were small, we tried caravans one year, without success. Diane found them difficult to tow, and everything I touched seemed to fall apart: for example, under the sink I assumed the knob led to cutlery and was stiff, but when I gave it a good tug, it came away in my hand. It was false. The bed also collapsed.

Turning to tents, we set off for Campbeltown, but no place seemed to please. It was too windy, too many people, too few people, too many midges, and, halfway down the Mull—in desperation—I stopped for a fag. Far below lay some tents. I knew whose tents they were, but Diane did not. After spending the winter in Campbeltown the travellers moved up the Mull collecting whelks.

I pitched the tent on the other side of a head-high clump of ferns and the first Diane became aware of our neighbours was when a wee, dirty, naked boy hurtled through the ferns and started doing cartwheels and handstands in front of the tent. Too late in the day to move, Diane banned me from joining a riotous ceilidh that our friends behind the rushes had that night.

§§§§§

The first time I was in the USA was a week's course on *Professionals and Drink/Drugs* in Salt Lake City, Utah. I was not in rehab (too expensive), but learning how to recognise and help the afflicted in my own field.

En route, I met a man called Joe in London; he was ramrodding the AA show for the rest of the UK. I overdressed for my appointment with a lovely cream Noel Coward suit, $400 shoes and a cravat. I looked so lovely, but I added the see you Jimmy hat[1] just for the final touch. Now, desert boots, a kilt, rugby shirt, and a See You Jimmy hat is OK, but dressed up like Little Lord Fauntleroy is very, very scary. I donned my bonnet as I left the Scottish flight and wandered about Heathrow for a couple of hours. It was terrific. If I caught someone looking at me, I'd smile in a sort of mad fashion with my

---

[1] tartan bonnet with bright red hair

head to one side. People nearly broke their necks looking the other way, or to catch sight of my attendant psychiatric nurse.

I loved the Americans, especially the ones from the Deep South, because you don't have to explain *double entendre* or sarcasm to them. On the last day of the conference, the morning session was *Sex in the Dental Surgery*. I set two alarm clocks and was there in the front row an hour early. The session broke up acrimoniously as the dental surgeon giving the lecture upset some people for various reasons, one of which was using real glamour models to demonstrate the possible arising issues from an unchaperoned surgery and dental chair.

The final afternoon's lecturer was a friend of ours. Joe and I had plotted to burst onto the stage wearing the see you Jimmy hats, and do a turn to relieve the finale and say our goodbyes.

'We can't do it now,' Joe said, 'We'll be lynched; there's too much bad feeling left over from the glamour model session.'

We had rehearsed the night before and decided not to waste it, especially since the bonnets had cost me a fortune. As well as making us look dashing, they played the tune 'Bluebells of Scotland'.

We charged onto the stage, pushed Dr X aside and went into that old favourite from college days, 'My father's a pervert in London, my mother makes bootlegger gin …'

It was met with the total silence of about two hundred wide-mouthed American doctors and dentists. My partner in crime started to falter and I could see myself having an early bath when, thanks be, they understood our farewell capers and laughed.

Just as I was saying goodbye, a huge monster of a man came up and drawled, 'Lachlan, it's been a pleasure to meet you—you're a God-damned hooligan.' That is probably the nicest thing anyone has ever said to me.

§§§§

46 Dentists in Greece Left to right: John Watson, Iain Appleyard, AMF, John Sinclair, John (Jock) Linton, Howard Hobbs

§§§§§

Continuing in holiday mode and taking early retirement, I went round the world, visiting my numerous rellies on the way.

First step was cousin Colin in the Bahamas. He had been a Governor of Abaco, and then a big noise in Grand Bahama—impressive. The Bahamas had been a popular entry port for drugs. Having survived the Bahamas Airline, I lined up at passport control and immigration. The officer addressed a point one foot above my left shoulder and intoned, 'Sir, are you carrying any drugs of firearms?' Resisting the chance to reply, 'only ten kilos of heroin, and an AK47,' I replied a quiet 'No.' At this point, a huge officer covered with pistols and a club approached. He asked me, 'Are you Lachlan Buchanan MacDonald?' Resisting the chance to follow my 1950s movie star heroes who would doubtless answer, 'Who's askin', Bud?' I said 'Yes,' very quietly.

'Follow me,' he boomed.

I did as I was told, imagining cries from fellow travellers of 'drugs baron', visions of airless cells, chains and a fate worse than death filling my mind. Around the corner was Cousin Colin. One of his little jokes; it runs in the family.

Overeating in the Bahamas, I left with a stomach the size of a beach ball and farted my way across the Pacific. It was not a pleasant flight for anyone sitting near me. Surprisingly, at my next destination I was met by a relative, another cousin, who had not driven outside his own small village for about twenty years. He had only one arm which worked, but had felt obliged to meet me at Melbourne Airport. The horror of this journey back was superseded only by his shoving a live grenade into my lap as I dozed off in his home. 'It's OK,' he said reassuringly, 'the trigger is strapped down with black tape, and I keep it in my glass cocktail cabinet.' Welcome to Australia.

Apart from getting lost up a mountain as darkness fell at Hope's Gap, things were good until I met the man from Sydney. Going to an AA meeting, I was hopelessly overdressed again. The other patrons wore shorts and singlets, bare feet optional. I was walking back to my digs, and this man engaged me in conversation at traffic lights, which seemed to take hours to change.

'Hi, are you a visitor?' (With the amount of clothes I was wearing, I was either a visitor or a nutcase.)

Being told I was a visitor, he asked me if I would be in Sydney next week. I replied no and my new companion said,

'That's a pity. It's the gay and lesbian Mardi Gras.'

I dropped my voice an octave, and replied gruffly, 'I'm awa' hame tae Scotland the morn!'

'Have a nice day,' he said, and gave me a friendly dig in the ribs.

I skedaddled off to the YWCA. When I had arrived, the day before, I apologised for getting it wrong, I had meant to go to the YMCA. The receptionist drawled through her gum, 'We take all kinds here,' and they certainly did.

Off then to Cairns, or as the Aussies say, Cannes, and on to the Great Barrier Reef. Three months before, they had left two people out there, and all they found in the morning was a pair of flippers. The guide lectured us on Great Whites, box jellyfish (they kill you quickly, apparently) and getting scratched by the poisonous corals on the way out. I was having second thoughts about snorkelling until the crew—mainly young women in black bikinis—appeared. Hell, I couldn't let the clan down, so with, 'perhaps today is a good day to die', I threw myself over the side with some alacrity.

§§§§§

I arrived in Tokyo in a snowstorm and was met by my daughter Seònaid. We drove across Japan to Jōetsu City, and the next day I awakened to a blizzard and snowdrifts. This city faces Korea and Russia, and is surrounded by mountains, so I donned all my clothes and went to buy more.

First day, my daughter left me beside this huge ice-cream machine in a store. I had just bought an ice-cream. You can buy anything out of a machine in Japan. I bet if you know where to go, a little Japanese girl called Honda *bheag* (means 'wee' in Gaelic) will slide down a chute, and cry, 'Hello, Sailor! Welcome to Japan!' I noticed a Japanese girl of three or four in full kimono and she was smiling at me and pointing to the ice-cream dispenser. What to do? I can't speak Japanese and it's my first day in a foreign country. I curse the modern pervasion of fear of dealing with children in public. Thirty years ago, I would have bought her an ice-cream and entertained her with farmyard noises until her mother arrived.

I usually go to see people rather than places, as I'm often disappointed in countries. Perhaps I build them up and glamorise them in my mind. I have never seen anywhere more beautiful than *Earra-Ghàidheal*[2] on a good day in Scotland. West is best on a sunny day, but then, I'm a wee bit biased!

---

[2] Argyll

HOTELS

The earliest hotel I can remember is in Edinburgh where Mother and I stayed whilst my father was in hospital there. We normally stayed with rellies when we ventured forth from the island, but not this time. It was the winter of 1947 and the cold was hellish in the establishment and in my bed. The white linen sheets were starched stiff like sheet iron that had been in a fridge and stretched so tightly over the bed that I had difficulty breathing. How I longed for Lismore with big coal fires and cosy flannelette sheets. Father recovered and lived for another twenty years.

§§§§

Holidays down the Costa del Plonk in the 1970s and 1980s were always good for a laugh. We landed at one hotel late at night, tired and emotional. The room was so small that we had to walk over the bed to get to the bathroom. I told my wife, 'I'll fix it after breakfast tomorrow.' The staff did not seem to have much English or Gaelic in this third-rate joint, and after breakfast I managed to lock us out of our room. Panic stations; in half an hour I had the manager who did speak English, a joiner with no English, a handful of cleaners, and a couple from along the corridor who loved the drama of the whole affair. Breaking into the room, I opened a couple of bottles of Black Label I had from Duty Free, and we all sat on the bed and had a small refreshment and a good party. Two hours later, we had a lovely balcony room at the front of the hotel.

I noticed a maid with a swollen face and, after putting her on an antibiotic, extracted a posterior molar. In these days, with children and a wife who was my finals patient at the uni and who has constantly needed dental treatment (if she had been paying me privately I could have retired young), I carried an emergency pack of dental gear.

We were adopted by a lovely young honeymoon couple from Fort William. The only respite we got was when we went to bed.

On another occasion, I became friendly with one of our UK rugby teams who were staying in a hotel across the way. Previously, I had watched them trying to destroy themselves by diving from a first-floor balcony into the pool and thought 'what interesting people'. I invited them back that evening to my room to meet the wife. It was two o'clock in the morning and my good lady awakened to find the inebriated forward pack of a Welsh rugby team all trying to get into the bedroom at once to say hello. At that point, I looked around and realised just how big rugby players can be, especially if you're asleep one minute and awake the next. I was not a popular person.

§§§§§

In 1994, and 50 years after our second invasion of France, Fionn's future in-laws and I went for a week to the Normandy beaches. Someone told Mama Betty (Kären's mum) about a good place in Cherbourg called the Hotel Duvet which sounded pretty cosy. Delayed and arriving at 10 p.m. we entered the thinnest building in the world and ascended countless stairs in a place whose last makeover was in 1946, after the bombing stopped. On every landing there was a large cupboard, holding—I imagined—a skeleton with goggles and flying jacket, aka Biggles!

The sheets were grey and I spent all night switching on the light and throwing back the bedclothes to catch the bed bugs (I was unsuccessful). In the morning I took off my drawers and *semmit*[1], rolled them in a ball, and threw them into the back court. I had contemplated setting them on fire, but with my luck would have probably set the place alight.

An ancient crone sat just inside the dining room door and watched us with beady eyes. My friendly greeting, *'Vive la France! Vive de Gaulle! Vive la kilt!'*, the only French I knew, was greeted with a look of pure hatred.

I sipped a bowl of ersatz coffee, presumably made from ground acorns, and fled into the Normandy mist. I afterwards discovered that an enormous rabbit which bided under the stairs was for our dinner that night. French cuisine?

---

[1] vest (undergarment)

§§§§§

On a tour round the world to see the rellies (the Irish and Scots frequent every nook and cranny of the known world), I naturally went to see two of the other Lismores: one in New South Wales, and one in Victoria on the Hamilton highway, both in Australia. The latter Lismore is a real one-horse town, and the hotel is a wooden one-storey building. I met the local editor and told her I was a dentist looking for rellies, but she gave me a spread in the local paper as a Scottish historian in search of his roots!

A lady with a houseful of antique prams wanted to see a video I had of Lismore, Scotland, and although her grandchildren told her that her daughter did not want us, she charged into her daughter's house with me in tow, banged the cassette into the television and watched it while her daughter continued to smoke and drink in the same room looking the other way. When the video finished, she left with me murmuring 'thank you' in her wake.

I fell worriedly asleep that night to the screams of a woman down the corridor shouting 'yes, yes!' Later, in the darkness, I was attacked by some large, winged creature and eventually threw myself and the bedclothes on top of it; it was a huge moth. The screams had stopped, so I spent the rest of the night listening to the possums crashing and dancing on the roof. It sounded like a herd of buffalo on drugs doing an eightsome reel. I had asked the apparently lone woman who ran the hotel to wake me at 6 a.m. for breakfast. She said in response, 'No chance, mate' and showed me to the kitchen.

Up country, the room in the Cairns hotel was small, windowless and had a fan on the ceiling that looked like a propeller from a World War II Spitfire and which spun violently, threatening to rip the ceiling off or lift me and the room way, way up and away. The room number was 33, and every time I asked for the key, the receptionist almost fell off her stool. Apparently it's the way I roll my Rs.

§§§§§

My wife organised a weekend up in her Pictish home territory and booked this flash, baronial pile on the internet. We arrived in the dusk of a winter's evening to this gloomy-looking, apparently empty, large house. After a prolonged ringing of the bell and banging the knocker on a huge door, a dishevelled Lurch-like creature appeared from the trees behind us and asked,

'What do you want?' We explained that we had booked a room. 'We are closed, but I'll see my sister.'

He produced a sister dressed in tweeds that looked as if she had slept in them; she had. We asked if we could have some food and she said, 'perhaps Granny could rustle up some soup.' I was for the off, but my daughter (made of sterner stuff—she had travelled all over the globe) said to hang on, it was all very interesting.

Things were not looking good, but it was late and the rooms looked normal, even if they had seen greater grandeur in the past. The TVs didn't work and the shower was a hit or a miss; the heavy drapes had seen service in World War II as blackouts and there were stuffed dead animals lurking in corners wearing dust for fur.

I was trying to fix the television in my daughter's room when there was a knocking on the wall from the room where my wife was having a lie-down. It was too loud to be deathwatch beetles; we thought it was a bit of family malarkey, so knocked back cheerfully. The knocking became more like panic, so I went next door. I found my wife stuck in the middle of a collapsed chair; all four legs had caved in, its heavy embroidered back and sides had pinned her to the floor, and she was unable to get up.

In the morning, I ran through the different disasters and asked for a rebate on the bill. She took £5.00 off and wistfully said, 'I don't suppose you'll be coming back then?'

§§§§§

I still use hotels and am ever-hopeful. I feel uncomfortable in B and Bs, cold in tents, and unsuccessful in caravans.

PS: I sleep best in boats; maybe it feels like being back in the womb.

THE POLICE

When I was young, we had no police on the island of Lismore, and no need of them. No-one locked their door anyway and mostly everybody behaved as directed by their parents, preachers and teachers—apart from the night that Big Donald stole Mary's 40-ouncer. Peace reigned and violence broke out only when necessary.

It was only when I went to high school in Oban at age 12 that I saw my first uniformed policeman on the beat. A policeman did come annually to Lismore to oversee the dipping of the sheep, to make sure there was no cruelty involved. I can recall passing him, sometimes weaving his way back to the ferry. It's a cold job, dipping sheep. I don't remember seeing many policemen in Oban. Perhaps it was the crowd I ran around with; we were not hooligans.

Father, who shot everything that moved and caught everything that swam, would occasionally go over to Kingairloch with a policeman friend and get us some venison. Father, like myself, used the word poaching to refer to the fact of dropping an egg into boiling water. I love the true story of the chap who was accosted by the landlord.

'These are my rabbits in your pocket.'
'Why?'
'Because this is my land.'
'Why?'
'My father fought for this land.'
'OK. I'll fight you for them.'

There is a beautiful sequence in the film *The Maggie*, when the agent is involved in the crew's poaching activities and is led off protesting as they go off on their merry way.

My first personal encounter with the force was in my first year at university when, after the official Bejants' Welcome[1], I discovered myself in the city centre of Dundee jumping up and down on the rubber lines of the traffic lights to make them change. We did not have traffic lights in Oban, which was the nearest big town, and even if we had needed them in Lismore, there was no electricity there until 1970. Suddenly two big Dundee cops appeared and asked me where I stayed, then told me to get to my bed before they put their boot up my a**e. Good advice!

§§§§

For five months in the summer of 1965 when I worked alongside the Irish and Highland Tunnel Tigers on the Loch Awe hydro scheme, I had been to the local dance and got accosted by some hooligans at the front door. Things looked bad for the boy from Lismore when suddenly a cop appeared out of the darkness saying, 'He's mine,' and threw me into the back of a police car. A little way down the road, he pulled into a quarry, produced a half-bottle from the dash and said, 'You'd better have a slug of that.' 'Oh God,' I thought. 'Out of the frying pan and into the fire.' Switching on the light, he said, 'You don't recognise me, Lan, but I knew you right away.'

It was an old boyfriend of my sister whom I had thought was terrific when I was a kid, because he could yodel, blow smoke rings and sometimes took me to the pictures with Margaret. Imagine taking a snotty 12-year-old with your sister on a date! He certainly saved my bacon that night, but sadly died of a heart attack looking for climbers up the mountains a year later. A lovely man, with a great sense of humour.

§§§§

One night, after exams, and after drinking, dancing and walking a girl home half-way to Arbroath, I was wending my way back to my lodgings in Dundee. I stopped at the Police Station and asked the desk sergeant if I could lie down in a cell for a few hours. Reclining with his feet up on the desk, he did not even deign to reply. He wordlessly pointed to his boot and then at the door. Thanking him profusely, I retreated into the cold dawn. Perhaps Dundee cops had a fixation between a boot and a *tòn*.

---

[1] Bejants are newcomer first years to Saint Andrews University

§§§§§

My future wife and I went to a Dundee Art College pyjama party. We became separated and she decided to go home. Having lost her coat in the muddle of the cloakroom, and mad at me for disappearing, she walked home in her nightie! She was stopped by the police on the way home. In horror of what her mother would say if she were taken to the police station at 1 a.m., she gave a first-class performance of sleep-walking! The police, being decent Dundee laddies, took her home to her flat. Lucky one there, then!

§§§§§

Qualified and working in Fife, I was singing a few Gaelic songs at a care home for the elderly, with my daughter (8) and my mother (80) for company. I had been celebrating Saint Andrew's Day the night before (a big night out) but had had nothing to drink at the ceilidh with my mother watching! On the way home. stopped by the police because I was weaving about the road, my daughter, a lovely little girl and always ready to help out, spoke up in defence from the back seat.

'Mummy says Daddy always weaves when he drives.'

Thanks, lovely girl. Then the cops asking me the registration of the car, she helped again. 'Daddy never remembers the number.'

So, just over the limit, I copped a year's ban. Waiting for the police surgeon for a blood test in the station, I spent a lot of time with the younger policeman speaking of independence for Scotland. At that time, I was Membership and Literature Secretary for the Scottish National Party (SNP), spokesperson and door-knocker. On that Sunday morning, while collecting my particulars, my policeman asked for a membership card, so the time was not completely wasted.

§§§§§

Time passed. I remained police-free, and then Fionn joined the Metropolitan Police in London: cadet training in Hendon for a year, then training in the Met and out facing all London could throw at him before he was twenty. Choosing an area of London where there would be lots of work for police, he had no wish to be a walking-talking tourist guide, as he put it himself.

He moved into a Met Police Section House in the middle of London. Parents could stay overnight there too for a small sum of £7.00, a good price. Most of the cops I met were London boys and a cheery lot: 'A shit, a shower, a shave and a bit of nose-bag mate!' The *craic* was terrific!

At my son's passing out parade dinner, he asked me to make a speech on behalf of the parents. Well, feeling safe away down there, I used my jokes about the Scottish police and I kicked the Strathclyde Polis uphill and down dale.

Back in the 1950s, there were so many Hielan' Polis in Glasgow that it was known as The Hielan' Mafia and there were many stories I could tell of it. For example, there was a new cop in Glasgow, and his uncle, the inspector, found him struggling to drag a dead horse around a corner into Hope Street. On enquiring what was going on, the new polis said the horse died in Sauchiehall Street but it was easier to spell Hope Street. Denigrating jokes re the Strathclyde force went down a treat with the Met, so I was feeling good!

Towards the end of the dinner, a middle-aged man approached and told me that his daughter was in my son's unit and she had her passing out today, too. I congratulated him, introduced myself and he told me who he was: the Chief Constable of Strathclyde Police. I lowered my head and held out my hands—clasped together.

My son married a lovely girl who was also in the Met Police Cadets. When I am with them I forget I have met the Met; maybe that's normal.

My wife and I are still very nervous of police wo/men coming to the door. Is there something wrong with my son or daughter-in-law? We shake in case it is bad news. Bellowing at them at the door, which one is it? They stagger back and tell us it is the next door's alarm.

§§§§

I am not the most observant of people and sitting having my breakfast in a big kitchen one day, my wife asked me if I had noticed anything different. Right enough, looking around, I noticed that windows were open, curtains billowing in the wind, all the cupboard doors and drawers were hanging open, the laundry bin was emptied on the floor, the back door was wide open. Oops, we've been broken into and burgled? Speaking to a nice young policeman later, I asked if there was any chance of this burglar being caught; it was a fairly small quiet town we lived in then. Yes, the youngster assured us, a very good chance because the police knew this chap's methods, or as the young man put it, his *'modis operatis'*! That was a relief then.

§§§§

From having eight police forces in Scotland, they changed it to one. In the last three weeks I have been stopped three times by the police for … wait for it … weaving. I have three theories:

1. I drive too close to the centre line, realise suddenly and correct it;
2. eyesight—astigmatism;
3. a growth on the left side of the brain which makes me change course to starboard!

My first stop was by *Weegie*[2] cops, who behave in the original John Wayne manner: with attitude. For some reason, I had a great desire to smile/laugh, crack gags or rap. When asked where I was going, I said Oban and started speaking in an Oban accent. This is loud, slow, and comes out in gale-like bursts of verbose with the accent/stress on the second syllable. I also adopted the half-smile, head to one side and loooong vowels much beloved of the isles folk. At one stage, the lead actor polis—sergeant—wanted me to breathe on him. I was so tempted to say no and claim halitosis or say, 'Gee, officer, we have only just met!' but saying to myself, 'Lachlan, get a grip,' I behaved.

The second duo were from the Perthshire force and I had my sister in the back of the car. She feels safer in the back when I am driving. I made the mistake of calling the front seat the suicide seat once; she's never forgotten. Normally, my sister talks a lot anyway, but with the cops there she went into high jibber. Included in this harangue were conspiracy theories, vindictiveness and accusations (since my son is in another police force). I sat with my head bent, hoping he would not test *her* for drink, drugs or eightsome reels; she's getting too old for dancing!

[2] Glaswegian

After listening to my sister not taking a breath for a while, the cop said to me, with the slow deliberation of a judge donning the black cap, he had come to the conclusion that my weaving was my sister's fault.

'You see, you have been forced into turning your head to answer your sister and this has caused the weaving. Keep her in the front seat,' was his advice as he b*****ed off. The younger policeman at this point leant heavily on my wing-mirror, which already had a wobble. It promptly fell off. Pausing only for a second in his conversation, the sergeant said to take the car along to the police station and they would fix it there.

The third lot of stopping polis were from Argyllshire and were intelligent, polite and courteous, as are all people from that county. I, of course, used my normal Argyll accent as they would have known I was taking the Michael. I mentioned that cops still make me nervous and one of them replied, that he and his mate were like that too, out of uniform. Looking at my licence he said, I see you are a doctor. I replied that I preferred to be called Mr as the only real doctors are those with a PhD, not just a courtesy title like the medics used. Smiling at his chum, he said, 'you should hear what some of those b******s call us.' Any more of this banter and we would all be off for lunch together.

47 Margaret at home in Lismore

§§§§§

On all occasions when stopped by the police and asked, 'when did you have your last drink?', my eager reply is—and it's all in the timing: 'I believe it was the end of April, 1983.' Long may it continue!

§§§§§

I know many cops gags, but I like the tale of the wee Gorbals lad who, when asked to write a story about the police, handed in his essay which said simply, 'The Polis are b******s.' The teacher reprimanded him and organised a day out for the boy with the police with a drive in a squad car, a trip around the gaol, and a large ice-cream. On asking for another essay on his treat, he wrote, 'The Polis are cunning b******s!'

§§§§§

There is a thin blue line protecting me from the hooligans. There are 20,000 fewer cops in the UK now than in 2010. At least Maggie did notice, but then she was taking on Scargill and the unions at the time.

Sleep easy!

OLD AGE

Cha tig an aois leatha fhèin
Old age does not come alone

Don't I know it! I used to stride like a ranging timber wolf, but now it's a mincing shuffle like a *seann chailleach* [1].

Who was it that said, 'There are many things to be said for growing old and right now I can't think of one of them'? Rubbish! That's just an old man's gag. Of course there are: grandchildren, friends and rellies, some 'sense and mental' tapes full of songs, poems, ditties and quite interesting knowledge.

Not a great deal of veneration for the elderly is left; mind you, is it our own fault for giving too much attention to the little darlings?

Mother had the right idea; on high days and holidays, she would say gently in Gaelic, 'You'll be needing a good thrashing by the end of the day, so we'll do it now and get it over with!' (Just a wee gag, Mother.)

The old are valuable: silver in our hair, gold in our teeth, gas in our stomach and lead in our boots. Unfortunately, the memory goes.

My minister often says, 'Lachlan, you must think more of the hereafter.'

I reply, 'Minister, every time I walk into a room, I say, 'now what am I here after?'

The Chinese say that as you grow old your ancestors come to visit so you get to look like them. The Scots say that if you look at your mother-in-law you'll see what your wife may look like in forty years' time; but if you rearrange 'mother-in-law' you get the words 'Woman-Hitler' (sigh—Ed).

Now we come to the bit we have all been waiting for all of our lives: death.

---

[1] (old) old woman

> My candle burns at both ends;
> It will not last the night;
> But ah, my foes, and oh, my friends—
> It gives a lovely light![2]

I don't give a lot of thought to the future or the past, unless the black dog comes upon me. The curse of Scotland: lack of confidence and fear of failure. It's mostly the things I have not done or attempted that worry me most. Och well, yesterday's history, tomorrow's a mystery and all I have is today.

I have said in my will that my ashes are to be scattered around the *cairn* at the Kilcheran islands off Lismore because I have taken so much fish out of there that it's only fair that I restore some of the nitrogen.

Another trick with ashes is to make them into a timer so that I'll go on working for the banks and the taxman even after I'm dead!

I'll have a piano accordion playing Gaelic waltzes and family songs, and just as the curtains close, a hand with a huge diamond ring and waving a red silk hankie will be my final farewell as the massed choir sings a rousing 'Wish Me Luck as You Wave Me Goodbye', or maybe 'Goodnight Ladies, We're off to Sea Again.'

I just hope it's not a cold place (I should have been born in the Med, and no gags, please) and I can run like a 12-year-old again in my new sandshoes over there in *Tìr nan Òg*[3].

Amen!

---

[2] Edna St. Vincent Millay, 1892–1950
[3] Land of the Ever-young

SKETCHES

The Alkie

CHARACTERS

MALKIE	A recovering alcoholic, highly nervous, paranoid chap
NEILIE	A gently-spoken, withdrawn man who keeps to himself

SETTING

The same close (tenement), top two flats. On one side lives MALKIE, and on the other, NEILIE. It's MALKIE's turn to cut the communal green for the close and his grass-cutting machine has broken down. The distance between these men's two front doors is ten feet and the thought process which follows takes as many seconds.

MALKIE

(muttering to himself) It's ma turn tae cut the grass and ahm no' spendin' guid money on fixin' that auld machine. Mibbe the guy across the loaby will lend me his. Mind yi, he's a teuchter fae the Hielans, an' they heuchter teuchters can be funny buggers at times. Ah never see him doon the pub, an' ah dinna trust a man wha disnae drink. He speaks thon ither Gaelic stuff. Ah've heerd 'im gabbin' awa' at it tae himsel' when he's pittin' oot the bin. He speaks posh Scots tae, but ah bet he gangs tae the lavvie like the rest o' us dae. He'll ask me why dinna ah get mines mended; ahm no gonnae tell him ah cannae afford it and let masel' doon in front o' the likes o' him, stuck-up bastard! Ahv a guid mind tae punch oot his lichts!

(MALKIE rings his neighbour's bell. NEILLIE answers it.)

NEILLIE
(quietly) Hello.

MALKIE
Ya Hielan' hoor. Ah widnae borror yer machine if it was the last ane oan the planet!

The Close

CHARACTERS

HENPECKED MAN	A wee, timid soul who lives on the first floor of a Glasgow tenement is getting hell from his wife because the new tenant on the ground floor has a dog which *cacs* [1] in the close.
BIG HAIRY MAN	A new arrival who, amongst other distinguishing features, is missing finger on the left hand which has changed the tattoo on that hand from 'hate' to 'hat'.
DOG	A huge Rottweiler whose droppings have made the close into an obstacle course for the residents.

SETTING

The ground floor of aforementioned tenement. The upside of the arrival of the heavenly twins in this particular close means that the druggies and alkies have vanished from this, their usual haunt.

(Timid knock at the door of the new tenant's flat)

DOG
(growls)

BIG HAIRY MAN
Come in and dinna mind the dug; he widnae hurt a flea.

---

[1] defecates

> HENPECKED MAN
> I'm a bit feart o' big dugs, though.

> BIG HAIRY MAN
> (smugly)
> It's OK; this wan is only trained tae defend.

> HENPECKED MAN
> Ah jist cam doon tae welcome ye tae the neebourhood.

> BIG HAIRY MAN
> Thanks a lot. Fancy a beer, neebour?

> HENPECKED MAN
> No thanks, the wife disnae like the smell.

> BIG HAIRY MAN
> That's OK. Ahd nae intention on kissin' her onywey. That's jist a wee joke. Ahm a helluva man for gags!

> HENPECKED MAN
> (hesitatingly) It's aboot the close.

> BIG HAIRY MAN
> Whit aboot the close? It's a fine close, no' like ony a thay fancy, wally closes in the 'Shields[2] or in Guffan[3].

> HENPECKED MAN
> Weel, ahm nae worrid for masel; but the wife objects tae the droppings; no' that ahm blamin' you, mind.

---

[2] Pollokshields, an area of Glasgow
[3] Govan, an area of Glasgow

BIG HAIRY MAN

God min, if ah dumped like that, ah'd be on the telly, *Freak or Unique*? (laughs heartily)

HENPECKED MAN

Aye, they are quite a pile. The last time the wife stood in one, she was up tae her knees in it!

BIG HAIRY MAN

(proudly) Weel, he's a big dug.

HENPECKED MAN

The wife says, can you no' tak him for mair walks?

BIG HAIRY MAN

His back legs are givin' oot, and ma knees are knackered; (sadly) we're no getting any younger, the pair o' us.

HENPECKED MAN

(with a mild show of courage) The wife thinks he's an (imitating wife's posher accent) 'awfae ugly doag'.

BIG HAIRY MAN

(without rancour) Christ, she's wan tae talk wi' a face like a skelped arse; I'd no tak' hame an unopened wage packet tae that yin.

HENPECKED MAN

Aye, it's nae been easy ower the years. (sniffing mournfully into his hankie) She's at me fae morning' tae nicht.

BIG HAIRY MAN

Ach, ye poor wee bugger. Ye'll at least admit that we've got rid of the alkies, druggies, hoors and comic singers fae this close.

                    HENPECKED MAN
Aye, I ken, but the wife says …

                    BIG HAIRY MAN
Aw awa tae hell wi' the wife. Tell ye what: let's get rid
o' her.

(Scene fades with HENPECKED MAN and BIG HAIRY
MAN, new best mates, heads together, discussing strategy.)

The Dug

CHARACTERS

POSTMAN — New to the area and with a parcel to deliver

LADY OF THE HOUSE — Upper crust and a bit offhand with more important things to do than tend to the servants

SETTING

A very grand, large house with a rolling lawn and high walled gate at the front. There is a large aggressive looking mastiff sitting under a bush near the gate. The POSTMAN rings the bell. The LADY OF THE HOUSE answers the intercom.

POSTMAN
Hello, it's the Postie wi' a big parcel for yi.

LADY OF THE HOUSE
Just bring it up to the front door, please. I'm just getting out of the bath.

POSTMAN
It's the dug, Mrs. I dinna like big dugs.

LADY OF THE HOUSE
He's just a baby, really. Afraid of his own shadow.

POSTMAN
Aye, he looks it. (stares hypnotically at the slavering jowls). I'll just leave it at the gate here.

> **LADY OF THE HOUSE**
> (forcefully) No, it's valuable and there are lots of common people about.

> **POSTMAN**
> The dug's standin' up noo, growlin' and showin' his teeth, Mrs.

The LADY OF THE HOUSE appears at an open window in a white dressing gown and her hair wrapped in a towel turban.

> **LADY OF THE HOUSE**
> If he comes near you, just kick his balls; he'll leave you alone then.

> **POSTMAN**
> Pardin?

> **LADY OF THE HOUSE**
> Kick his balls for him. He loves it.

> **POSTMAN**
> (fearfully and worriedly) Are yi sure aboot this?

> **LADY OF THE HOUSE**
> Perfectly, I do it all the time for him.

Reassured, the POSTMAN slips through the gate with the parcel, the dog approaches him, he gives the dog a mighty kick in the appointed place. There is an awful howl of anguish and the dog goes into attack mode. The female voice from the window drifts down exasperated but really unconcerned.

> **LADY OF THE HOUSE**
> Oh you shouldn't have done that; I meant the *rubber* balls he plays with in the garden!

Bha daoine càirdeil san eilean àghmhor,
A chuireadh fàilte oirnn nuair bha sinn òg:
'S e dhèanadh feum dhuinn a dhol air chèilidh,
A dh'èisteachd sgeulachd nan daoine còir

> *There were friendly people in that happy island,*
> *Who would welcome us when we were young;*
> *It gave us pleasure to go visiting,*
> *And hear the stories of the fine people.*

'An t-Eilean Àlainn'
Seumas Dòmhnallach

LADIES I HAVE KNOWN

Having enjoyed Colin Tindal's article, 'Boats I have Owned', and with apologies to my forefathers, here are a few verses on *Ladies I have Known*.

The Skiff or Rana 1

You were a 15-foot skiff built in the Norwegian fashion
Your rake, sheer and thrust spoke of blonde men with axes
With four oars you flew.
In you, the children in red suits learned to row;
Now, like me, you are growing old; perhaps I loved you best of all.

48 *Rana 1*

Hurley 20

They called you a yacht but you were really a big dinghy with a lid.
I sold you to an Englishman who grew mushrooms for a living.
No racehorse you;
Wee, wet and tender,
I searched for you one morning in Glenuig, but you had gone.

Hurley 22 (with compliments to McGonagall)

Fareweel wee Hurley 22, you've aye been dear tae me,
Many a night you've saved my skin on a dark night off Tiree
The north wind roared, my bum was sore
And the furrow followed free (apologies—Coleridge, 1798)
But the Captain said, 'Ach haud yer wheesht, we'll soon be home for tea!'

49 Fionn with *Salvo* (1992)

50 *An t-Each*

On An t-Each (The Horse)

You were a Centaur but had two keels and did not sail well to windward,
You had a kind of chunky beauty and were bright and cosy for your length.
'Boys' toys,' the women say.
Part horse, part man, and now she is called *Grace*.
My grandfather had a smack called *An t-Each*, but she was a workboat.

The New Boat: Fumarole

You are called a Westerly Fulmar, a sharp beak and a big fat *tòn*[1],
'As tender as a woman's heart,' my father used to say
And I did not know why he laughed,
Tobruk[2] and Baghdad[3] are always big and full
And Rudolph Hiss[4] has no patches
But at night I dream of the widow-maker's boom[5].

Rana 2

New, clean and white and your name is Euisbree[6].
'Low maintenance' the man said but they say lots of things:
'She runs like a Singer sewing machine and just sips diesel;
diesels like to be worked hard; just keep changing the filters.'
She was bought for the children and is OK in a blow;
But, she's made of plastic
And I can't feather my oars.

---

[1] backside
[2] water tank (terms taken from the old boat)
[3] fuel tank (terms taken from the old boat)
[4] rubber tender
[5] a low-slung boom to catch more wind but was liable to smack you in the head
[6] *Euisbree*: to incorporate all the grandchildren: Euan, lssy, Brianna

Meander: Colvic 28

You spent your youth as a houseboat on the Clyde
A covered-in cockpit and carpets in the saloon
'A boat fit for an older man'
My wife said
Now in your maturity, you spread your wings
And bare your breast to the Western rollers.

51 *Meander*

LAN'S DITTIES, RAPS AND DOGGEREL
Mainly for children of all ages

With apologies to my forefathers, James, John and Lachie MacDonald, and *Lachann Dubh a' Chrògain*, but if you invite me for tea, I'll sing them for you.

I get bored very quickly, which means everything in this book is very short, which is probably a great relief to my readers. Here are some ditties, raps and doggerels which are even shorter.

A Sailing to Ireland 2006
To the tune: 'Oh My Darling, Clementine'

CHORUS

In the bilges[1], in the bilges,
Pumping water every day
Is it fresh or is it salty?
Everybody had their say

VERSE 1

When we left on Monday morning
It was blowing from the west
I was feeling rather chilly
So I donned an extra vest

VERSE 2

I had on flotation clothing
Bought in haste for Scotia's shores
The insulation was a godsend
The rest were soakit[2] to the pores

---

[1] People always say if there is water in the bilges:
'Is it fresh or is it salty?'
'I don't know.'
'Taste it, then.'
'Don't be bloody silly, I know what's in there: salt water, fresh water, diesel, urine and probably *cac*. Taste it your bloody self.'
[2] soaked

52 Robert Watt, sailing companion of many years

VERSE 3

Malin Head was in the distance
The wind was rising by the hour
Bob the Builder3 on the tiller
Dreaming of secluded bowers

VERSE 4

John the Dentist at the compass
Directing passage through the mist
Longing for a friendly harbour
And a chance to get real pissed

---

[3] My sailing companion for many years of frightening the life out of me. He says his boat is better than mine and is also reluctant to sail in my boat as he says it's a dangerous bloody thing He's probably right!

VERSE 5

Lach the Liosach, guts were churning
As he hummed a cheery air
All the time his heid was spinning
He couldn't really tak much mair

VERSE 6

Safely berthed in Galway Harbour
The boys were feeling pretty fine
The journey back was filled with action
Under this, I'll draw the line

CHORUS

In the bilges, in the bilges,
Pumping water every day
Is it fresh or is it salty?
Everybody had their say

Santa's a Scotsman

Tune: Lan's own tune (you'll need to buy the CD!)

CHORUS

Santa's a Scotsman, his beard is snowy white
His nose is red, like Rudolph's, 'cos he's always on the skite
Up in Ballachulish, he makes the children's toys
And fires them doon the chimney for the little girls and boys

VERSE 1

Big Mary's a helper, and so are all the elves
Goin' like the clappers and filling all the shelves
'X days to Christmas,' I hear the punters shout
Nae money in the pocket, and the plastic's up the spout

VERSE 2

The turkey's in the oven and the sprouts are on the stove
The tension here is rising, we're really on the move
Mama Scotland's on the warpath, and really on a roll
It's time to leave the kitchen, and take a little stroll

VERSE 3

The job is nearly over for yet another year
We're stuffed right up wi' goodies, and almost out of beer
The punters all are skint now, there's sorrow in the glen
But if the big man spares us, we'll do it all again

CHORUS

Santa's a Scotsman, his beard is snowy white
His nose is red, like Rudolph's, 'cos he's always on the skite
Up in Ballachulish, he makes the children's toys
And fires them doon the chimney for the little girls and boys

On Precenting in a Gaelic church

The noise is eerie, like an African chant or a Mosque in Bangladesh
My father presented in the *Earra-Ghàidheal* fashion:
Musical and uplifting.
But this is a death chant
No redemption for me
Oh well: buy a blue suit
Join the church
And hope that God has a bad memory

'Puter in a Surgery

They call you a PC but half the world can see
That's not personal.
You sit in the corner waiting,
Like a beast before it strikes;
The operator hypnotised like a rabbit by a stoat.
Some say that you will rule the world—
But I hope I'm off by then

Reflections at a Surgery Window

The surgery is clean and white and antiseptic
In striking contrast to the dark, sooted buildings across the street
The mini trees in the chimney have lost their leaves
They will blossom green in the spring again
But the people and shops speak of a poor desperate nation

On Seeing Theresa May for the First Time, 2016

Theresa May's got a big nose
Where did she get those chi-chi clothes
Oh my god, it cannot be true
It's Maggie and Denis Thatcher, Mark II.
Be afraid, be very afraid

Theresa May, Christmas 2018

Theresa May's here to stay
No matter what happens
She won't go away
Boris Johnson mouthing off
What else do you expect
From a big fat toff

Theresa May 2019

Theresa May's up in the air
And some folk crying it's just no' fair
She's coming and going like Old King Cole
But still we're in a bloody great hole

'Brexit, wrecks-it,' the punters cry
And all the stories are a bloody great lie
But bet your boots they'll escape this farce
While poor Jock Tamson's flat on his a***

Ah Wanna Be a Trendy Leftie
Tune: Lan's own tune

VERSE 1

Ah's got cars in the garage, shares in the bank
Twixt Tony and Labour, we gotta walk the plank
The Liberals are finished now, if they only knew
With cock-up after cock-up, they're really in the stew

CHORUS

Ah wanna be-e-e-e a trendy leftie

VERSE 2

We wrecked the education, many years ago
When back there in the '70s we cried, 'go, go, go, slow!'
The Unions ruled the roost then, till Maggie came along
But when she wasted Scargill, we sang a different song

VERSE 3

She spoke of market forces, and put millions on the dole
Destruction of the working class seemed to be her goal
We weren't really worried 'cos we now were middle class
Those socialist hardliners, we'll put them out to grass

VERSE 4

The pensioners are dying now, thousands every year
One coal fire, or one-course meal, there's never cash for beer
They say we are champagne socialists, what's wrong with being rich?
It's better than my dear old Dad who used to dig a ditch

VERSE 5

Our kids now go to public school, we used to call it private
Our holidays are Costa Plonk, we never go to Margate
Our accents changing every year, you'd almost call them funny
Who cares if we are hypocrites, we're right there in the money

VERSE 6

Things don't look so good now, they've caused an awful stink
And leaning even further right could end them in the clink
We'd cosy up to Gordon if he didn't look so sour
But bet your boots we'll be alright, whoever comes to power

CHORUS

Ah wanna be-e-e-e a trendy leftie

Rap

About a week before the 2014 referendum on Scottish independence, a well-known socialist appeared as a guest speaker at a meeting in Ballachulish Hall. He had discovered that MacDonalds, Stewarts and Camerons are buried on Eilean Munde, and compared this to the different political shades who were voting SNP. Smart boy.

> Jonny cam tae oor wee toon
> Cryin' 'vote for SNP!'
> Some o' us been doing that since 1963
> 'Whaur's yer Red Flag noo, ma man?'
> Cried Wattie fae the back
> 'That game's a bogey,' Jonny cried, 'go stick is up yer cra**.'

53 Eilean Munde

The Englander

Once we sailed free; size, race, religion or creed a nothing
Proud of a British sea heritage; admired and feared by others
Suddenly the world has changed
Big boats—small minds—
The price of everything and the value of nothing
Now in the West, an Englishman's pontoon is his castle

O seinn mun dealbh seo, a chlann nan Gàidheal,
Lios Mòr na h-Alba, fo dhìon nam beann;
'S ged dh'fhàg sibh 'n t-àite, na caill bhur cànan,
'S gum bruidhinn sibh Gàidhlig ma thig sibh ann

>   *So sing about this picture, children of the Gael,*
>   *Lismore of Scotland, under the shelter of the mountains;*
>   *And though you have left, do not lost your language,*
>   *So that, should you return, you will speak Gaelic there*

'An t-Eilean Àlainn'
Seumas Dòmhnallach

REFLECTIONS

THE MACDONALD CONNECTION

My father knew we came from Glencoe and said that we were blood-connected to *Iain Abrach*[1], but this was *beul aithris*[2] and before DNA. Now we know that James MacDonald left Glencoe in the late 18th century and came to Port Ramsay in Lismore.

This James can be traced back to Alexander MacDonald of Achtriachtan, a tacksman who was alive in 1692. In the clan system the tacksmen were cousins, or closely related to the chief. The last of the Glencoe chiefs in the direct male line was Major-General Alexander MacDonald, who died in Teddington, England in the 1840s (1776–1840).

The MacDonalds of Glencoe were a small sept compared to the MacDonalds of Glengarry or Clanranald who could put thousands on the battlefield. The area of Glencoe can only support about 500 to 600 people, as can be seen by the numbers out in the 1715 and 1745 risings: about 100 to 150 fighting men under MacIain.

The Glencoe Massacre had its birth the year before in 1691, when many of the Highland chiefs met at Achallader (ruined house before you climb up to Rannoch Moor) and some of them agreed to back the Hanoverians rather than the Stuarts. They had to sign this before 1 January 1692. MacIain, the chief of Glencoe, delayed this until the end of December, and mistakenly thought he signed it at Fort William where the troops were, instead of Inveraray. On the way to Inveraray, a long way in thick snow, he was waylaid at a Campbell castle in Appin. The Campbells accepted his late signature and he returned home, thinking all was well. However, the decision was made in London that an example had to be made of these savages. What a marvellous excuse: '… that the old fox, nor none of his cubs get away. The orders that

---

[1] original chief of Glencoe MacDonalds
[2] oral tradition (word of mouth)

none be spared from seventy, of the sword, nor the Government troubled with prisoners.'[3] An attempt at genocide by the English government failed for a variety of reasons and I'm still here.

The Union of the Parliaments in 1707 was followed by the Jacobite risings of 1715 and 1745, bringing the destruction of a whole culture, and leaving the Gaels in complete chaos.

The Proscription Act of 1746 took away the right to dress in tartan, wear a kilt, play bagpipes (the war pipes), carry weapons (even for hunting) and to be caught speaking Gaelic could have serious consequences.

At one blow, many of the symbols by which a culture identified itself were swept away, and to be caught using them could and—in some cases—*did* mean transportation or death. After the demoralisation of the Highlands came the Balmoralisation of the Highlands[4]. Rule Britannia, Britannia rules the waves, with three small corvettes, two destroyers and a nuclear submarine. This is getting heavy, and remember the leitmotif of this book is PNI. So …

People still have a gathering in Glencoe, and every year I have this debate whether to support it or not. On the one hand, but on the other hand …

The religion of the Glencoe MacDonalds, and indeed of that whole area (count the Episcopal Churches), was—and is—Scottish Episcopalian, which is not to be confused with that south of the border. It can be argued that the Scottish Episcopal Church has the most direct link to that of Saint Columba's in Iona.

Some say that the religion of Iona was that of love, and the religion of Rome is that of laws. Don't get me started on tonsure: shaving of the head. Instead of shaving the crown, you shave the front. I saw a chap like this one night and engaged him in conversation thus:

'So interested to see you're using the old Celtic tonsure.'

'Whit?'

'Your hair.'

'Ach the front was straggly, so I cut it off.

Twixt two cultures again. Maybe I *am* an alien (see the television programme *Third Rock from the Sun*).

---

[3] McDonald, D, Clan Iain Abrach a History of the Macdonalds of Glencoe (2012)
[4] MacDonald, D (1994) The Cultural Construction of an Island Identity—An Ethnographic Study of an Inner Hebridean Island on the West Coast of Scotland (Doctoral Thesis, University of Stirling)

I myself abhor resentment and the fact that I have 13 February 1692 tattooed on my chest is pure coincidence! The Gaelic/Scottish community is often blamed for dwelling on past glories, real or imagined. *'Wha's like us? Damned few, and the buggers are a' deid.'*

Only the historian who understands the present can understand the past. Well, that lets me off the hook, being a dentist. Twixt two cultures yet again. Hand me a pill; the headache is coming back!

54 The nearest DNA matches so far.
I love it that the kilted ones from USA and Australia are in Highland dress and the locals, Alasdair and I, are in more casual attire!
(Photograph: *The Oban Times*)

CLOSING

If you think this chapter is all about drink and fornication, you will be disappointed, since I was at my work as well! I had my first alcoholic drink at the age of 18 and my last at 43. In the summer before university, I found a job as a labourer on the Lismore Pier, tarting it up. It needed it badly, having been built in the previous century. One day, whilst loading aggregate at Point, a supply of alcohol found its way over from Port Appin on the mainland. I didn't refuse a glass of whisky, and a wee heavy. Twenty minutes later, it hit me! The feeling was magnificent. Almost like an altered state of consciousness (whatever that is), but you ken what I mean. That was me, not hooked but hugely interested and perhaps a bit in love with the effect. This became a habit before events, using alcohol as a prop-up medicine for many years until finally, after 25 years, I crashed and burned!

Now for my own personal explanation. I was quite good at shinty and athletics but I had no ball control for football. I developed a technique which involved sprinting straight into the opponent with the ball, and after two or three collisions, if I was not sent off, the opposition managed to get rid of the ball before I arrived. I suppose it was a form of rugby/soccer, and from what I have seen of the modern professional game, it has arrived.

Recently, they have discovered that running produces an ingredient of THC[1] (wacky baccy, a very convoluted substance, which gives a high). That is why dedicated runners, and not necessarily professional sportspeople, will run in all weathers, even when they are ill. I also produced lots of adrenaline and excitement, which climaxed on birthdays, Christmas and New Year celebrations. As previously explained, my mother would say first thing in the morning of an exciting day to come, '*Lachuinn*, you'll need a good thrashing before the day is out. We'll do it now and get it over and done with!' 'Oh

---

[1] Tetrahydrocannabinol, one of the cannabinoids

thank you mother, you are so considerate!' My mother never once caught me, but I can still hear her shouting, 'I wish I was ten years younger; I always caught your sister!'

Add lots of dopamine, which is the body's natural feel-good factor, and acts positively with alcohol in at least 10% of people, now add dancing and pretty girls to the mix, and it surprises me that I didn't go into orbit!

One in ten people are at risk, but only one in ten of these get and stay sober. These are not good odds! As my sponsor used to tell me: 'If you are alcoholic and keep drinking, there is a very good chance that you will have an early, painful death, be admitted to a lunatic asylum, or end up in nappies.'

Having said all that, alcohol affects one physically, mentally and spiritually, as well as being cunning, baffling, and powerful. There is help out there if you want to find it. It ranges from the medical profession to other bodies like The Council for Alcohol, and AA (Alcoholics Anonymous). Personally, I have been in the AA since 1983, worked with the GDC (General Dental Council) for some years, and in that time I have met people who claim to have become sober through their own methods such as sport, religion, love and sex—of course not all at the same time (I am open to suggestion, as the bishop said to the actress).

It all seems to boil down to one single factor, and that is: staying away from one drink, for one day at a time, it's impossible to get drunk. Illicit drugs have a huge amount of publicity—rightly so—but it is alcohol which gives the police, the medical profession, and the family and neighbours most grief. Legalising drugs, as we have done with alcohol and tobacco, seems to be for some the way forward, but it also has its pitfalls. How in the name of the wee man (whoever he may be) could we organise manufacture, control and distribution when we cannot even agree to leave or stay in the EU!

Anyway, I am giving up on politics (as well as the booze), apart from Scotland's First Minister, whom I admire immensely! My generation had it so good; if you had the ability and—importantly—were given the right push by the right people at the right time, then twenty years of free education was not to be sneezed at! I have poked fun at Scottish people, including myself, all my life but I am getting serious now and this will have to stop.

As well as staying away from one drink, for one day at a time, be grateful, laugh, and if you can't do that, learn today—at once! I have also been lucky in understanding and using three languages; Gaelic, English and *Lallans* (known often as *braid Scots*). Having been brought up as a liberal thinker due entirely to my parents, teachers and preachers, I have come to accept *Lallans* or *braid Scots* as a language in its own right. Over the years I have asked academics (who usually sit on the fence anyway—what's new?) and in the majority of cases they say it is.

§§§§§

There are many books which have been written about Lismore by people who have lived and died there, or are living there now, or even just visited. (note: there are several Lismores in the world, including two in Australia and another in Ireland).

The *Book of the Dean of Lismore* (beginning of 16th century) was collected and compiled by Sir James MacGregor, a church dignitary and Gaelic scholar. He also had a poet brother, Donnchadh, who was involved in this work.

Alexander Carmichael (1832–1912), who was born and buried in Lismore, collected and collated *Carmina Gadelica* (1900) There are now in existence six volumes of the collection, but only the first two were written by Alexander; the other four by his daughter, grandson, and another two academics. This book covers words, rites, prayers, poems and customs, orally collected in the Outer Hebrides, mostly South Uist.

The Very Reverend Iain Carmichael DSO and of the same family as Alexander Carmichael wrote *Lismore in Alba* (1948), a book packed with information and interesting facts about Lismore, much of which is ecclesiastically-based. The author told my father that winning his DSO in World War I was a lot easier than writing the book!

A close relative of my own—my wife Diane—an anthropologist, completed a thesis of Lismore in the early 1990s, looking at *A Cultural Construction of an Island Identity*, which followed the view posited by Tomás Ó Criomhthain originally from his exemplary book, *The Islandman* (1929): '… to set down the character of the people about me so that some record of us might live after us, for the like of us will never be again.'

The late Alastair Livingstone, Baron of Bachuil (a hereditary title, as the family are the keepers of the black staff of St Moluag in their home on Lismore) was for ten years chairman of the 1745 Association and was a joint editor of the book *No Quarter Given: The Muster Roll of Prince Charles Edward Stuart's Army, 1745-46* (2001). This deals with the Clans who were out for Bonnie Prince Charlie (Stuart) in the 1745 Jacobite Rebellion ending in defeat at Culloden Moor in 1746. It is an amazing amount of work for the three editors to have completed.

My sister, Maighread MacDonald Lobban, in her book *Lachann Dubh a' Chrògain'* (2004) (Dark Lachlan of Croggan), one of the bards of Mull and Lismore, covers our great-grandfather from Mull and his grandsons from Lismore, Lachie, John and James, the last being my father. This book concentrates on their *bàrdachd*[2], although an article of Margaret's, called 'Growing up in Lismore' printed in *The Scots Magazine* (1995) gives a good picture of life in a ceilidh house before World War II.

My cousin Donald M Black (*duine uasal*[3]) in his book *Sgeul no Dhà às an Lios* (*A Tale or Two from Lismore*) (2006) gives us a marvellous taste of an island community from the inside. Donald, the brother I never had, was born and bred in Lismore and was, of course, bilingual. He was a farmer on the island, as well as being a top Scottish athlete when he was young. Donald was also my personal counsellor, mixing wisdom and calmness with good common sense when my imagination ran away with me.

Another author, Robert Hay, living in Lismore, tells of the early days to the present in an enjoyable book called *Lismore: The Great Garden* (2009). He is a professional scientist in agriculture and gives an in-depth analysis of farming on the island. More recently, he described the island's experience of the Clearances in *How an Island Lost its People: Improvement, Clearance and Resettlement on Lismore, 1830-1914* (2013).

Lismore is awash with talented writers, and New Zealander Pauline Dowling has continued both Lismore literary and seafaring traditions by writing of her travels with her husband Captain Stuart Ross in *Going Bananas: My Trailing Career (Volume 1)* (2017).

In recent years, Helen (Eilidh) Crossan has recorded some of the Gaelic-speaking *Liosaich* talking about their lives, as well as editing audio-visual contributions for the *Comann Eachdraidh*.

§§§§§

Following on from the above, Culloden, the last battle to be fought on British soil was a serious mistake. It was doomed from the start and had serious long-term and continuing consequences for the Highlands and its

---

[2] poetry
[3] gentleman

people, as did the Massacre of Glencoe (1692). Although it was not really a 'massacre', the point of it being so well-remembered in Scottish history was that the English, Lowland Scots and even some Highlanders who were in the British Army were ordered to kill as many clansmen as possible. The Campbell leader and his men had accepted Highland hospitality for several days, only to arise in the night and kill their hosts. This was breaking the age-old hospitality tradition of the Highlands. It was, and still is, looked upon with horror.

Another huge historical event which happened in the nineteenth century and which had a devastating effect on the Highlands and Islands was the decade-long Highland Potato Famine which started in 1846; this was an echo of the Great Famine which was infamous in Ireland for killing a million people between 1845 and 1852.

The Highland Clearances were also in progress by the 1840s, people turned out of their wee houses, often with the family cow kept in the but and ben, as the house was known. With few possessions and little money, the landlords wanted to put more sheep on the land instead of Highlanders and Islanders. There was more money in sheep.

The Clearances certainly had a huge effect on Lismore, with the population going down from 1,400 souls in 1840 to fewer than 200 in the time I went to school in 1945. The south end of the island died and has never recovered.

I was visiting Dunrobin Castle a few years ago. The Sutherlands who owned these lands and castle were infamous in their clearances of their own kin. I was speaking to some friends who were with me, and having a rather loud voice, I was saying, 'I suppose you could look at the Clearances as giving the clanspeople a new start; there was plenty of wood in Canada to build houses, and generally speaking the natives were friendly over there!' I was ignored by the twee official guide ladies in their tweeds who were keeping a close eye on me in case I lifted anything. A man from the island of Harris who was working there realised I was taking the mickey and engaged me in conversation.

The Royals come up from the South in August to shoot things in the Highlands; the local people line the roads to stare at them. 'Bloody rude, you'd have thought their mothers would have taught them better manners!' (Royals or locals? You choose—Ed.)

§§§§§

This is difficult: ending a book of stories about me and my family that I have loved and do love now. I attended Celtic Connections in Glasgow last year and a young man sang love songs my father used to sing. He won a Gold Medal at the Mod a few years ago and he had the same musical, light, tenor voice my father had. I was suddenly taken with a warm, happy feeling and was very conscious of the presence of my forefathers; it was very pleasant and made me feel we should have no fear of the hereafter.

An t-eilean àlainn san Linne Mharbhairnich,
San d'fhuair mi m' àrach nuair bha mi òg -
Nach tric mi smaointeachadh ort am aonar
Gun toir mi gràdh dhuit gach là rim bheò.

The beautiful island in the Linn of Morvern,
Where in my youth I was reared—
Often I think of you when I am alone
And I will love you every day of my life

'An t-Eilean Àlainn'
Seumas Dòmhnallach

ABOUT THE AUTHOR

Lachie B's Greatest Hits

Born: 15 June 1939, Isle of Lismore

Age
10 Burst Appendix
12 Missed femoral artery by 1"
16 Motorbike crash
25 Fell off bus and burst arm
25 Nearly drowned at Appin
25 Catapulted through car sun roof
25 Got married
26 Qualified
27 Lump on groin removed
43 Stopped alcohol
49 Heart attack
54 Quadruple bypass
61 Varicose veins removed
71 Basal cell carcinoma (head) removed
77 New knees
78 Retired

55 Who's a lucky boy then?

Never mind nine lives, I have used up nineteen. The sensible thing would be to sit beside the fire and smoke my pipe, but then I'd be dead before the salmon run again. *Gus am bris an là.*[1]

---

[1] Until the day breaks

www.ingramcontent.com/pod-product-compliance
Lightning Source LLC
Chambersburg PA
CBHW071956070526
44583CB00015B/1211